Block

Ultimate Beginners Guide to Mastering Bitcoin, Making Money with Cryptocurrency & Profiting from Blockchain Technology

By Stephen Satoshi

This books contains 2 Manuscripts:

Cryptocurrency Beginners Bible

Blockchain Beginners Bible

Table of Contents

no scenarios in which the publisher or the original author of this work can be in any fashion deemed liable for any hardship or damages that may befall them after undertaking information described herein.

Additionally, the information in the following pages is intended only for informational purposes and should thus be thought of as universal. As befitting its nature, it is presented without assurance regarding its prolonged validity or interim quality. Trademarks that are mentioned are done without written consent and can in no way be considered an endorsement from the trademark holder.

Financial Disclaimer:

I am not a financial advisor, this is not financial advice. This is not an investment guide nor investment advice. I am not recommending you buy any of the coins listed here. Any form of investment or trading is liable to lose you money.

There is no single "best" investment to be made, in cryptocurrencies or otherwise. Anyone telling you so is deceiving you.

There is no "surefire coin" - one again, anyone telling you so is deceiving you.

With many coins, especially the smaller ones, the market is liable to the spread of misinformation.

Never invest more than you are willing to lose. Cryptocurrency is not a get rich quick scheme.

Cryptocurrency Beginners Bible - How You Can Make Money Trading and Investing in Cryptocurrency

"The ones who are crazy enough to think they can change the world are the ones who do". - Steve Jobs

"The stock market is a vehicle to transfer wealth from the impatient to the patient" - Warren Buffett

Introduction

In just 7 short years, the value of Bitcoin has increased from $0.08 to over $4000[1]

In just a single year, Ethereum's price rose from $11 to $395 and back down to $295 at the time of writing.

The current cryptocurrency market is worth around $130 billion, more than the total GDP of countries like Hungary and Kuwait.

These investment returns are completely unprecedented from any traditional stock or index fund using fiat currency - which is precisely why the cryptocurrency universe is exploding.

---

[1] Source: Coincap.io - 2017 price as of 22/08/2017

We have daily news articles perpetrating "Bitcoin value could reach $5000 by 2018" and yet 2 results further down on a Google search we have a contrary article with the headline "Bitcoin value has peaked says Billionaire."

In the month of July alone we saw predictions of Ethereum being at $1000 by the end of 2017, and other commentators speculating that the value would plummet to just $50 in the same time period.

It's safe to say - there's a whole lot of hype out there

This book is designed to separate fact from fiction, we want to take a step back from the hype and look at the fundamentals of some of the more prominent cryptocurrencies to examine their viability as both as technological entity and as a trading/investing vehicle. This is to give you a well rounded view on whether these coins have potential for you to make money - which many of them do

For reference purposes, I will refer mostly to Bitcoin when talking about general cryptocurrency technology and using cryptocurrency as a means of exchange. Further, in-depth explanation of Ethereum and other altcoins can be found later in the book.

What is Cryptocurrency?

Depending on who you ask, defining cryptocurrency will elicit answers from "the money of the future" all the way down to "the biggest bubble since the DOTCOM bubble". US senator Thomas Carper summed it up best in laymens terms.

"Virtual currencies, perhaps most notably Bitcoin, have captured the imagination of some, struck fear among others, and confused the heck out of the rest of us."

For a more accurate definition, cryptocurrencies are simply currencies that do not have a centralized lender like a country's central bank. They are created using encryption techniques that limit the amount of monetary units (or coins) created and then verify any transfer of the funds after their creation.

This creation technique is known as "mining" due to its theoretical similarity to mining gold or other precious metals. To mine cryptocurrency, one needs to solve an increasingly complex computer algorithm or puzzle. Solving these algorithms takes a lot of computer processing power, and consequently, electricity. In other words, it costs money to mine them, so we can't just create value out of thin air. Therefore these currencies and their value are secured by the laws of mathematics as opposed to any central government or bank.

As cryptocurrency adoption increases, so does the number of real world uses. Everything from physical goods, gift cards, tickets to sports games and even hotel bookings can be purchased using cryptocurrency. Certain bars and restaurants have now also started accepting it as a means of payment. A number of NGOs now accept donations in Bitcoin and other cryptocurrencies as well. There are also more illicit uses, with the cases of underground online marketplaces dealing in illegal goods, such as Silk Road and AlphaBay.

These currencies have a huge number of advantages versus the currencies that we know and use today. This is what makes them so attractive to both long term investors and short term speculators. Of course, like any investment, cryptocurrencies do indeed have some potential drawbacks to them - and we will examine these later on in this book.

An Extremely Brief History of Cryptocurrency

While the practical applications of cryptocurrencies date back a mere 7 years, the technical aspects actually date back a further 30 years to the 1980s. Cryptographer David Chaum was the first to theorize a cryptocurrency when he invented an encrypted computer algorithm that allowed secure, unalterable exchanges between two parties.

Chaum later founded DigiCash, one of the first companies to produce units of currency based of his algorithm. It's important to note that only the DigiCash company, could produce the currency, which is a model unlike Bitcoin and other cryptocurrencies where anyone can mine the currency (providing they have the necessary computing power). After running into legal problems and rejecting a partnership with Microsoft that would have seen DigiCash paired with every home Windows operating system, the company went bankrupt in the late 1990s.

Chinese software engineer Wei Dai published a white paper on "b-money", which laid the foundations for the architecture behind the cryptocurrencies that we know today. The paper included information on complex algorithms, anonymity for purchasers and decentralization. However the currency itself never came to fruition.

US based E-Gold was another failed attempt at creating a cryptocurrency in the 1990s. The Florida based company gave customers e-gold "tokens" in exchange for their jewelry, old trinkets and coins. These tokens could then be exchanged for US dollars. The website was initially successful and there were over 1 million active accounts by the mid-2000s. One E-Gold's pioneering strategies was that anyone could open an account. However, this led to a number of scams being run through the website. In addition, poor security protocols led to large hacking incidents and the company went out of business in 2009.

The modern cryptocurrencies that we know today began with Bitcoin, which was first outlined by anonymous entity (the identity has never been confirmed as a single person or group) Satoshi Nakamoto. Bitcoin was released to the public in early 2009 and a large group of enthusiasts began mining, investing in, and exchanging the currency. The first Bitcoin market was established in February 2010.

In late 2012 Hosting and website development platform Wordpress became the first major retailer to support payment in Bitcoin. This step was key as it gave the currency real world credibility and showed that large corporations had confidence in it as a currency.

Cryptocurrency vs. Traditional Currency

Currency 101: The value of any currency is determined by what someone will give you in exchange for said currency.

Currencies, crypto or otherwise need to follow three basic rules:

1. They need to be difficult to produce (cash) or find (gold or other precious metals)

2. They need have a limited supply

3. They need to be recognized by other humans as having value

Using only Bitcoin (BTC) as an example, it ticks the boxes of all three of these characteristics:

1. Bitcoin uses complex computer algorithms in its production which take a lot of computational power, so it cannot be replicated easily or at a discount

2. There are a finite supply of Bitcoins - 21 Million to be exact[2]. As of 2015, roughly 2/3 of this number had been mined

3. There are hundreds of Bitcoin exchanges and Bitcoin is accepted everywhere from Subway to online dating sites

Where cryptocurrencies differ from traditional currencies (also known as fiat currencies) is that

---

[2] The actual supply numbers are measured in Satoshi (0.00000001BTC). There are 2,100,000,000,000,000 (2.1 quadrillion) Satoshi.

they are not tied to any one country, nation or institution (in most cases). There are no USA bitcoins, no Japanese Litecoins or any country specific altcoin. This is known as decentralization.

We also have to remember that fiat currencies that we know and love were not always the main players in the currency world. For centuries, Gold and other precious metals were seen as the most desirable currencies for day to day usage. It was not until governments could standardize and verify the metallic content of coins (and later paper bills) that they became the go to choice for citizens.[3]

Bitcoin was designed as a "deflationary currency" - meaning over time its value will, in theory, inherently increase. Unlike fiat currencies which

---

[3] Until rappers start rhyming about Bitcoins and Satoshis rather than Dollar Bills, Fiat will be the dominant form of currency

are inflationary and whose value will eventually decrease. After all, in 1917, $1 was worth the equivalent of $20.17 today. So the US Dollar is worth 20 times LESS than 100 years ago. In other words, if you continue to hold $1 over the course of 100 years, you will be able to buy progressively fewer and fewer items in exchange for it, whereas with Bitcoin, in theory, the opposite will happen.

As another real world example. On 22 May 2010, Laszlo Hanyecz made the first real-world cryptocurrency transaction by buying two pizzas in Jacksonville, Florida for 10,000 BTC. Today 10,000 BTC is worth over $40 million.

Bitcoin was designed this way so that no single person (or government) could increase the supply of money, lowering the value of the money already in the market.

Legendary Economist John Maynard Keynes had this to say about inflation and inflationary currencies.

"By a continuing process of inflation, governments can confiscate, secretly and unobserved, an important part of the wealth of their citizens. By this method they not only confiscate, but they confiscate arbitrarily; and, while the process impoverishes many, it actually enriches some. The sight of this arbitrary rearrangement of riches strikes not only at security, but at confidence in the equity of the existing distribution of wealth."

While Bitcoin has an air of uncertainty about it, based on the decentralization principle - where the real potential lies is in seeing it from the opposite perspective. With no single body being responsible for the supply of money, it forces all players (government, businesses and consumers) to be transparent about their processes, lowering the risk of fraud or tampering. The transparency is ensured by rewarding miners for their efforts (in the form of coin). This single dominating factor is why so many investors are confident about the long term viability of the currency.

One common argument made by Bitcoin detractors is that as there is no government backing the currency, it could totally collapse in theory. However, we have seen these happen numerous times with fiat currency under scenarios of hyperinflation where governments can no longer ensure the value of their money and as such have to create an entirely new currency. Common examples include the German Weimar Republic in the 1920s, where the currency lost so much of its value, that banknotes were used as wallpaper. Currently, the Venezuelan economy is on track to experience over 1000% inflation for the year, leaving many citizens unable to afford daily necessities like bread. Bitcoin enthusiasts see the cryptocurrency as recession-proof.

The cost of international transactions is another area where cryptocurrencies maintain a huge advantage over traditional ones. Anyone who has ever had to send money overseas will know that the cost of processing these transaction can reach ridiculous levels. There are times when these fees can top 10%. As cryptocurrencies do not view international transactions (as there are no "nations" involved) any differently from local ones, there are minimal fees for sending money to any part of the world.

The speed of transactions across borders is also much faster than regular fiat currencies, a Bitcoin transaction takes around 10 minutes to register as opposed to days for international bank transfers, and other coins process transactions even faster.

Understanding Blockchain Technology

So with no central lender like a Government backed bank, how is all this money worth anything at all? This answer is blockchain technology. If you plan to invest any money at all into cryptocurrencies, it is vital that you have at least a basic understanding of blockchain technology and its uses.

Blockchain technology allows for a permanent, incorruptible record of all transactions that have ever taken place, free from human errors or data loss. The important thing to remember is that these transactions do not always have to be financial, they can be in the form of legal contracts, auditing consumer goods and file storage.

Blockchain is essentially a giant database that is not stored in a central location. A floating database if you will. Because it is not stored in any single location, transactions recorded on the blockchain are publicly accessible and verifiable. We again go back to the idea of decentralization, and not having to rely on a single person or government to ensure our transactions will be safe.

In more practical terms, imagine all your financial information was stored on a single spreadsheet, not particularly safe right? Even if you had online and offline backups, these would be just 2 or 3 points of failure. What blockchain allows for is that spreadsheet to be shared across thousands of databases and continuously refreshed meaning that any changes would be recorded and no hacker could corrupt it at a single point of entry. As there is no single point of entry, there is now no single point of failure either.

Blockchain technology could be used to transfer everything from cryptocurrency, to tangible assets such as property without having to use a middle man such as a bank or other financial institution. This has potential to save consumers and businesses billions of dollars a year that are spent on transaction fees. While Bitcoin has gathered more mainstream press with regards to consumers, blockchain technology receives more interest from businesses.

How does Blockchain relate to Bitcoin and Cryptocurrency?

Bitcoin is not blockchain and blockchain is not Bitcoin or any other cryptocurrency. Bitcoins or other cryptocurrencies are transacted over a public network that runs on blockchain technology.

Blockchain is the underlying technology that allows bitcoin and other cryptocurrency transactions, but as previously mentioned - blockchain technology has many more potential uses. You can think of blockchain as an operating system, and Bitcoin as one of the hundreds of applications that run on that system.

Bitcoin and Cryptocurrency Drawbacks

Lack of Financial Regulation and The Ability to Fund Black Market Activity

One of the biggest strengths of cryptocurrencies is also a weakness in the system. The anonymity they provide allows them to be used to facilitate large scale black market operations and their usage for purposes of money laundering. For example, Silk Road - an underground dark net marketplace acted as a black market for illegal drugs. Payments were made in Bitcoin to protect the anonymity of buyers and sellers. The site was shut down in 2013 after amassing roughly $1.2billion in revenue. Founder Ross William Ulbricht was convicted of 8 charges and sentenced to life in prison.

Another nefarious use of cryptocurrency is in ransomware. Ransomware refers to malicious software that hackers install on a user's computer, then demand payment in Bitcoin to unscramble the software and allow the victim to access their data again. Ransomware schemes gained in popularity as using cryptocurrency as a means of payment means the people behind the attacks can seamlessly receive their ransom without revealing their identity.

Hackers

The elephant in the room regarding cryptocurrencies, with any early stage technology (which cryptocurrency very much is) there are bound to be breaches in security. Hackers have been responsible for some of the largest dips in the cryptocurrency market.

Tokyo based Bitcoin exchange Mt. Gox suffered losses of over $27.2 million and users lost over $460 million worth of Bitcoin after the exchange was hacked in 2011. At the time it was the largest cryptocurrency exchange on Earth. Amid talk of lazy management, and poor security protocols, the exchange ended up going bankrupt after the hacking incident.

Bitfinex, a Hong Kong based exchange was hacked in 2016 and its customers lost roughly $72 million worth of Bitcoin.

It is important to note that any hacking incidents regarding Bitcoin or other cryptocurrencies were done at the exchange or wallet level - not at the technology level. For further information on how to safely store your cryptocurrency, visit the wallets section of this book.

Data Loss and Human Error

If properly secured, cryptocurrencies will facilitate a shift away from physical cash which can degenerate and erode over time. As the data is encrypted and stored online, there is no way anyone (bar hackers) can access your funds.

However, this theory assumes perfect accountability from the user. As you may have figured out by now, none of us are perfect. We lose things. For example, we can lose our private encryption keys if they are stored on paper, or devices can become damaged or stolen if we are using physical encrypted wallets (like USB wallets).

Speculation and Misinformation

As previously mentioned, Bitcoin, and cryptocurrencies in general are a frontier technology. As such, mainstream media outlets, many of whom do not employ experts in the field, are liable to present misinformation regarding the technology, and the market itself. Blanket statements such as "bitcoin is better at being gold, than gold" do nothing but undermine the technology in the long run - but do make good soundbites for mainstream media

In June 2017, the Ethereum market briefly crashed after unsubstantiated rumors, perpetrated by 4Chan, claimed that founder Vitalik Buterin had died in a car crash. The hoax caused the market value to drop by around $4 billion in under 24 hours. This demonstrates that the volatility of the market in general is subject to manipulation by nefarious forces.

If you are planning on trading cryptocurrencies, you must be willing to experience sharp drops and rises in the market, far larger movements than traditional stocks. This is where being a rational trader will help you tremendously.

China

China's relationship with cryptocurrency is unlike any other country. No single nation has done more for the success of cryptocurrency than the Middle Kingdom itself. Cryptocurrencies are popular among Chinese investors due to the government's strict controls on their fiat currency, the Yuan. The biggest one of these being their currency devaluations, which hurt its value for trading and investing purposes.

This has led to many private individuals, both wealthy and non-wealthy, looking for alternative ways to grow their wealth. Cryptocurrencies are viewed by many as a more stable asset when compared to traditional investments. China's large quantity of cheap energy has also made it a hotbed for the cryptocurrency mining scene, which is now financially out of reach of most regular Western

European or Americans. Around 70% of the global cryptocurrency mining scene is located in China.

China is also liable for mass information manipulation. Mistranslations, rumour-mongering and coin pumps are all more susceptible in the Chinese market due to the lack of availability of foreign media - especially in the cryptocurrency space. In June 2017, the People's Bank of China (PBoC) issued a statement addressing false reports that the central bank was issuing cryptocurrency itself. The reports were thought the be part of a pyramid scheme to gain investors under the false pretense of a government backed cryptocurrency.

Survivorship Bias & Gambler's Fallacy

Contrary to what you may be seeing on internet forums & social media. There are people who have lost money in cryptocurrency. It's simply a matter of buying and selling at the wrong time.

It's the same reason casinos continue to do so well in part, the winners brag to their friends and family, while the loser stay silent.

Remember: **Never invest more than you can afford to lose**

This cartoon from XKCD sums it up perfectly.

NEVER STOP BUYING LOTTERY TICKETS, NO MATTER WHAT ANYONE TELLS YOU.

I FAILED AGAIN AND AGAIN, BUT I NEVER GAVE UP. I TOOK EXTRA JOBS AND POURED THE MONEY INTO TICKETS.

AND HERE I AM, PROOF THAT IF YOU PUT IN THE TIME, IT PAYS OFF!

EVERY INSPIRATIONAL SPEECH BY SOMEONE SUCCESSFUL SHOULD HAVE TO START WITH A DISCLAIMER ABOUT SURVIVORSHIP BIAS.

How to Buy Cryptocurrency

There are two ways to buy cryptocurrencies, the first is to use fiat currency (USD, EUR, GBP etc.) to purchase cryptocurrency via an exchange. These exchanges function the same way as regular foreign currency exchanges do. The prices fluctuate on a daily basis, and like regular currency exchange markets - they are open 24/7. These exchanges make their money from charging a small fee for each transaction.

Some charge both buyers and sellers, some only charge a fee for buying. For security reasons, most of these exchanges will require you to verify your ID before allowing you to purchase cryptocurrency.

It is also important to note the type of payments each exchange supports. Some allow for debit/credit card payments whereas other only accept paypal or bank wire transfers. Below are the three biggest and reputable currency exchanges for purchasing BitCoin, Ethereum and other altcoins with fiat currency like US dollars, Euros or British Pounds.

Coinbase

Currently largest currency exchange in the world, Coinbase allows users to buy, sell and store cryptocurrency. Coinbase is undoubtedly the most beginner friendly exchange for anyone looking to get involved in the cryptocurrency market. They currently allow trading of BitCoin, Ethereum and LiteCoin using fiat currency as a base. Known for their stellar security procedures and insurance policies regarding stored currency. The exchange also has a fully functioning iPhone and Android app for buying and selling on the go, very useful if you are looking to trade.

If you sign up for Coinbase using this link, you will receive $10 worth of free Bitcoin after your first purchase of more than $100 worth of cryptocurrency.

http://bit.ly/10dollarbtc

Kraken

Based in Canada, and currently the largest exchange in terms of volume of buys in Euros, Kraken has the advantage of more coin support (they also allow the purchase of Monero, Ethereum Classic and Dogecoin) than Coinbase. It allows margin trading, which while beyond the scope of a beginner, will be of interest to more experienced traders

For other cryptocurrencies such as Dash and Golem, you will need access to an exchange that facilitates cryptocurrency to cryptocurrency trading. The best one of these is Poloniex.

Poloniex

With more than 100 different cryptocurrencies available and data analysis for advanced traders,

Poloniex is the most comphrehensive exchange on the market. Low trading fees are another plus, this is a great place to trade your Bitcoin or Ethereum into other cryptocurrencies. The big drawback of Poloniex is that it does not allow fiat currency deposits, so you will have to make your initial Bitcoin or Ethereum purchases on Coinbase or Kraken.

How to send BTC from one exchange to another

If you're interesting in buying altcoins that are available on Poloniex or other exchanges for BTC, then you will first need to deposit BTC onto one of these exchanges. To do so from your Coinbase account click the "send/request" button and follow the steps below

1. Enter the wallet address of the account you're sending it to (e.g. your Poloniex BTC wallet address)

2. Select the correct Coinbase account that you are transferring funds from (e.g. your BTC wallet)

3. Enter the amount you wish to send

Cryptocurrency Guide

Beyond Bitcoin, there are a vast number of currencies emerging. Some with different characteristics and advantages over Bitcoin itself.

In this section we will examine many different cryptocurrencies and the fundamentals behind them in order to give you the best possible concise information regarding each one. The prices of these coins range from <$1 to over $300 per coin so there's something for everyone here.

One additional note to remember, is that cryptocurrencies are divisible, unlike regular stocks. For example, you cannot buy less than 1 share of Apple stock (currency $159.30). However, you can buy fraction of a Bitcoin or other cryptocurrencies. Meaning that even if you only have a small amount of cash to invest initially, you can still partake in the market, even if you can't afford an entire coin.

It should be noted that as of August 1 2017, Bitcoin and Bitcoin Cash operate as 2 separate coins. A further in-depth discussion of Bitcoin cash can be found later on in this book.

For each coin I have tried to list all major exchanges that list the coin as a purchasable asset. However, exchanges continue to list additional coins all the time. For a full up to date list of exchanges that carry your coin visit http://coinmarketcap.com

Things to Consider Before Investing in Cryptocurrency

It's not essential to know all the technical details behind a cryptocurrency before investing. However, answering some basic questions will help you decide whether you should invest in a coin or not. Here are some comprehensive questions you should know the answer to before delving into a currency.

- What problem does the coin propose to solve?

- How will the coin solve this problem?

- Why is this coin's solution the best solution out there? Is it the best solution?

- Who is the team behind the coin? What is their development history? How transparent is their code? Is it open source?

- Is there a public figurehead who will take accountability for any issues with development or adoption?

- Does this coin have competitor coins? If so, what is coin A's advantage versus coin B?

Bitcoin (BTC)

Price at time of writing - $4,070.13

Available on:

Fiat: Coinbase, Poloniex, Kraken

The coin that started it all is now one of the world's premiere assets. Sitting at a market cap of over $67 billion, the coin is worth more than global companies such as PayPal. We've already discussed Bitcoin in depth previously, so this section will discuss it for investing purposes.

With the price now sitting at a staggering $4,000 per coin, many commentators have claimed that owning Bitcoin is out of reach for the regular investor, but that's a stance I disagree with.

First of all, we have to remember that cryptocurrencies are not like regular stocks, in that they are divisible. So if you wanted to invest in Bitcoin, you don't have to purchase an entire coin. You can buy fractions of the coin so even if you only have $100, you can still get started in the cryptocurrency market.

Secondly, Bitcoin's deflationary designed role as a form of "digital gold" continues to make it the world's most valuable cryptocurrency. It also makes Bitcoin ideal to hold as part of your portfolio as many other currencies price movements are linked to it.

Another reason why any portfolio should contain Bitcoin is that if you want to purchase some of the lesser known cryptocurrencies, you will have to do so via exchanging them for Bitcoin as opposed to buying them outright for fiat currency.

Bitcoin Cash (BCH/BCC)

Price at time of writing - $326.77

Exchanges:

Fiat: Bitfinex, Kraken, Bithumb (ROK) ViaBTC (CN), Bter (CN), Huobi (CN), Bitcoin Indonesia (INR)

BTC: Bittrex, Poloniex, Cryptopia (NZ)

Bitcoin cash emerged as the result of a split or "hard fork" in the Bitcoin technology on August 1st 2017. The end-goal of Bitcoin Cash is to function as a global currency.

The split occured out of problems with Bitcoin's ability to process transactions at a high speed. For example, the Visa network processes around 1,700 transactions per second whereas Bitcoin averages around 7. As the network continues to grow, so do waiting times for transactions. BCC aims to run more transactions, as well as, providing lower transactions fees.

One of the major solutions to this issue is increasing the size of each block, so that more data can be processed at once. This is in line with solving the problems of scalability that Bitcoin was facing previously. The technology itself is worked in the short-term, with the first Bitcoin Cash block registering 7,000 transactions compared with Bitcoin's 2,500.

The success of failure of Bitcoin Cash will largely depend on Bitcoin's own adoption of the SegWit technology later this year, and the ability to process transactions quicker to act truly as a currency - rather than a speculative asset.

Detractors have also raised security concerns about Bitcoin Cash.

Bitcoin Cash has been widely adopted by many cryptocurrency exchanges. At the time of writing, there is only a few weeks worth of data available and thus, no one has been able to execute any long-term trends or technical analysis of BCH as a commodity. As further adoption continues, the price may well continue to rise. Early price rises for Bitcoin Cash have been largely driven by demand from South Korea, with over 50% of the total trade volume being seen on South Korean exchanges.

Miners have been quick to adopt the currency as well due to its higher mining ROI when compared to Bitcoin. The decrease in mining difficulty (leading to greater rewards for mining) will continue to see for miners move their resources from Bitcoin into Bitcoin Cash.

Note: Depending on your exchange, Bitcoin Cash may use the symbol BCC or BCH - double check before executing a trade

Ethereum (ETH)

Price at time of writing - $225.07

Available on:

Nearly every major exchange will allow buying of Ethereum for both fiat currency and exchange with BTC

If Bitcoin dominated the cryptocurrency space from 2008-2016, 2017 has undoubtedly been Ethereum's year. This relatively new cryptocurrency has made an immediate impact upon the space with some incredible technological innovations that have the potential to be groundbreaking, and game changing.

It is worth noting that Ethereum itself is not a cryptocurrency, it is a blockchain based platform. However tokens denominated as "ether" are traded on various exchanges. These tokens can be used for making payments on the Ethereum blockchain or exchanged for other cryptocurrencies or fiat currency. Many online articles will use the terms "Ethereum" and "Ether" interchangeably.

Where Ethereum shines is with a revolutionary technology known as "smart contracts". Dubbed by some as a technology that could potentially replace lawyers and accountants, these contracts are programmable contracts using blockchain technology, that can be set to execute automatically once a certain set of conditions are met. For example, an automatic deposit of 10 ether could be made into person A's wallet, once person A completes a task for person B. Person B has no way of breaking this contract once the conditions are met as the blockchain will enforce the conditions of said contract.

The potential applications for smart contracts are vast. From government, to management, to being able to set up a self-executing will, this is truly remarkable technology. A number of large international banks have already set up think tanks for technology like this, and adoption by any large institution has the potential to send Ethereum's price into the stratosphere. The Blockchain Banking Consortium project involves 43 international banks and aims to create a blockchain network that can enable large scale international fund transfer.

The platform is still in the development stage, and there are to this day, few real world examples of large scale Ethereum blockchain implementation. However, many investors have faith in the technology, which plays a big part in explaining the price rises over the course of 2017. In less than 1 month between May 18 and June 12, the price soared from $96.65 to a peak of $395.03.

Ethereum also suffered from a $4 billion single day loss in market cap after a hoax rumor regarding the death of founder Vitalik Buterin gained traction after originating on internet message board 4Chan. Let this example be another warning that cryptocurrencies are more susceptible to market manipulation than traditional assets.

Ripple (XRP)

Price at Time of Writing - $0.15

Available on:

Fiat: Bitstamp, GateHub

BTC: Poloniex, Bittrex, Kraken, Coincheck (JP), Bitso (MEX), Coinone (ROK)

The third largest cryptocurrency by market capitalization is one that flies under the radar of most investors and news sources. Launched in 2012 and acting as a payment network and protocol, Ripple aims to enable "secure, near instant and nearly free global financial transactions." Ripple transactions currently process in an average of just 4 seconds. The platform's ultimate goal is to make outdated payment platforms with slow transactions times and high fees like SWIFT or Western Union obsolete.

Many global banking institutions already use Ripple's payment infrastructure, including giants like BBVA, Bank of America and UBS. For example, using Ripple's payment platform, banks could convert currencies seamlessly, even for obscure countries and currencies such as a conversion of Albanian Lek to Vietnamese Dong. This would also negate the need for intermediary currencies such as US dollars or Euros. According to Ripple themselves, a switch to the platform can save banks an average of $3.76.

With adoption in the global banking sector, Ripple is off to a strong start. Especially if you look at it like you would a traditional startup.

Ripple also has the largest number of coin tokens (known as XRP) available out of any coin at 100 billion (39 billion available to the public), in contrast Bitcoin only has 16 million and Ethereum 94 million.

Unlike many open source cryptocurrencies, Ripple's source code is privately owned. The 100 billion coin supply was also "instamined", and in theory the owners could generate more at any given time, which would instantly devalue anyone holding coins. The central ownership is also at a clash with those who believe that cryptocurrency should be used as a force against one single owner. Researchers at Purdue University also determined that the platform had "security concerns", although as of writing, there have been no major incidents with the platform.

Dash (DASH)

Price at time of writing - $194.25

Available on:

Fiat: Bitfinex, xBTCe, Bithumb (ROK),

BTC: Poloniex, Bittrex, Kraken

Short for digital cash, Dash focuses on speed of transaction and anonymity as its 2 main selling points. Previously known as Darkcoin, it was rebranded in order to distance itself from the "dark web" of underground illegal cryptocurrency activity. Dash focuses on privacy, usability and the consumer market. Currently the coin fluctuates between the 5th and 8th largest cryptocurrency by market capitalization.

By speeding up transaction speeds from Bitcoin by using its Masternode network, payments are near instant versus the 10 minute waiting period for Bitcoin transactions. To obtain a masternode, users must deposit a total of 1,000 DASH. This had led to some debate about whether DASH is truly a decentralized currency or not.

Dash is less liquid than Bitcoin, meaning you may have a harder time executing large orders. However, the currency continues to be adopted by more exchanges every month. Dash's growth potential remains determined by its level of accessibility and adoption by the mass market. Once such example of this is BitCart, an Irish based discount gift card website which offers customers up to 20% discounts on Amazon purchases for payment in Dash.

Another interesting area in which Dash is utilized is the recent Venezuelan currency crisis.

Venezuelan Cryptocurrency exchange CryptoBuyer began selling Dash as an alternative to the local Bolivar currency which was, and still is, suffering from hyperinflation. Venezuelans are seeking to protect their savings, and cryptocurrencies like Dash allow them to do this by holding value against the US dollar.

Another area to note is that the richest 10 DASH holders currently hold 10.1% of the total coin value, which is almost double that of Bitcoin and Bitcoin Cash. This could have an impact if one of these major players wanted to influence market movements.

Monero (XMR)

Price at time of writing - $43.22

Available on:

Fiat: Kraken, HitBTC, Bter (CN)

BTC: Poloniex, Bitfinex, Bittrex, Bitsquare

Monero allows users to send and receive funds WITHOUT a public transaction record available on the blockchain. All Monero transactions are private by default. If you believe in privacy first and foremost, then Monero ticks all the boxes. The currency is designed to be fully anonymous and untraceable. This goes as far as their development team, which unlike other coins has no public CEO or figurehead.

Monero also uses "ring signatures", a special type of cryptography to ensure untraceable transactions. This allows users to receive money, without being able to link the address to the sender. This could be looked at as both a positive or negative depending on your viewpoint regarding anonymity. The ring signatures also conceal the transaction amount, in addition to the identity of the buyer and seller. Unlike Dash, Monero has been open source from its inception, so anyone can view the software code for total transparency.

The anonymity of the currency has made it a favorite of the dark web. Before its shutdown, darknet market site AlphaBay had adopted Monero as well as BitCoin to process transactions. Everything from illegal drugs, weaponry and stolen credit cards were traded on the platform. Its anonymity has also made Monero a favorite among ransomware hackers.

It remains to be seen if Monero will branch out to more legitimate use, such as to conceal one's true net worth. Or if it will continue to be the favorite coin of more illicit industries, preventing it from mass adoption versus other coins. This uncertainty could be used to speculator's advantage as they seek to profit from mass adoption potential.

Litecoin (LTC)

Price at time of writing - $40.11

Fiat: Coinbase, Poloniex

BTC: Nearly all exchanges support BTC to LTC transactions

The original altcoin, Litecoin has represented unglamorous yet steady growth in a cryptocurrency scene fueled by hype and large boom/bust cycles. Because of this, many analysts have deemed it the "low risk coin". Announced in 2011 with the intention of being "silver to Bitcoin's gold" and rectifying the shortcomings that Bitcoin faced at the time. Litecoin's coin limit is 4x the amount of Bitcoin's at 84 million coins making it too, a deflationary currency, The time to create a block is 2.5 minutes, a quarter of Bitcoin's 10 minutes. Litecoin was the long standing second purchases in fiat currency including Coinbase in March 2017, which was great news for US and EU investors. In terms of market behavior, generally Bitcoin and Litecoin follow a similar pattern in terms of increases and decreases in the currency value. Many investors choose Litecoin as a supplementary option to Bitcoin in order to diversify their portfolio.

For those interesting in mining, Litecoin's algorithm is far simpler which makes the mining costs and barriers to entry lower. Litecoin runs on the Scrypt algorithm whereas Bitcoin runs on the SHA-256. The main significance of this in practical terms is a lower mining cost as Scrypt is less intensive on Graphic Processing Units (GPUs). In 2017, Bitcoin mining is no longer a viable option for the novice or home based miner, whereas Litecoin mining can still turn a profit, even when factoring in electricity costs in first world countries.

Factom (FCT)

Price at time of writing - $19.71

Fiat: Coincheck (JP), Yuanbao (CN)

BTC: Poloniex, Bittrex

Like Ethereum, Factom expands on ways to use blockchain technology outside of just currency. While Ethereum is based on two way verification and ensuring contracts are unbreakable. Factom promises to do the same with large blocks of data by providing a record system that cannot be tampered with. This would allow businesses, governments to provide a track record of data without alteration or loss. The practical applications for this include legal applications, company accounts, medical records and even voting systems. Just imagine a world where it was physically impossible to rig an election, or where an accounting scandal like Enron couldn't happen again.

Like other projects utilizing blockchain, Factom cannot be altered because no single person runs the network. The network is collectively owned by millions of users, independently of each other. While data owned by one person is prone to malevolence, hacking, user error and alteration, the same is not possible with data owned by an entire network.

With regards to investing, like Ether is to Ethereum, Factoids are the "currency" of the Factom system. The more applications that are generated using Factom, the more these Factoids are worth.

Factom has already secured a deal with consulting firm iSoftStone to provide blockchain based administration software projects for cities in China. The deal includes plans for auditing and verification services.

Of the technology, Factom CEO Peter Kirby stated "We believe that this will help developers create a whole new class of accountable and tamper-proof business systems. This could be in insurance, financial services, medical records, or real estate – any system where record keeping is essential."

Like other blockchain technology, common questions surrounding Factom are ones of scalability and wider technology adoption. The other main drawback to Factom investing is whether the team can run the system at a consistent profit going forward - or whether the technology will lead to a race to the bottom in terms of price.

Neo (NEO)

Price at time of writing - $7.89

Available on:

Fiat: Yunbi (CN), Jubi (CN)

BTC: Bittrex, Binance

One of these earliest Chinese based blockchain projects, Neo, formely known as Antshares prides itself on being open source and community driven. The coin has been compared to Ethereum in the sense that it runs smart contracts instead of acting as a simple token like Bitcoin. The project is developed by a Shanghai based company called ONCHAIN.

In a June 2017 press conference held at the Microsoft China HQ in Beijing, the Antshares founder Da Hongfei announced the rebranding to Neo as well as some projects in the pipeline. These included collaborating with certificate authorities in China to map real-world assets using smart contracts.

Neo's base in China allows it unique access to the world's 2nd largest market and the largest cryptocurrency market which could be seen as a unique plus when compared to other cryptocurrencies. However current drawbacks include a limited number of wallets for the coin itself.

At the event - Srikanth Raju, GM, Developer Experience & Evangelism and Chief Evangelist, Greater China Region, Microsoft, said that ONCHAIN is "one of the top 50 startup companies in China." Support and positive press from a global powerhouse like Microsoft can only be a positive for Neo going forward.

Perhaps the biggest determining factor for NEO going forward is support from the Chinese government. While other cryptocurrencies suffer from legal battles with governments, Neo's relationship with the leadership has been low key if somewhat positive, with founder Da Hongfei attending government conferences and seminars on cryptocurrency and blockchain technology.

One thing to be wary of with Neo is once again, a Chinese factor. This time it's the language barrier, as much of the news about the coin is published in Chinese originally, there is significant potential for mistranslations in the English speaking world. For example, "partnerships" with Microsoft and Alibaba (China's largest eCommerce company) have been overstated due to poor translations from Chinese news sources. That doesn't mean collaborations like this aren't possible in the future though.

The smart contracts running on Neo include equities, creditor claims, bills and currencies.

Update as of August 2017: NEO is currently trading at $51.99 - in just a few short weeks a price increased of over 500%

Golem (GNT)

Price at time of writing - $0.26

Available on:

Fiat: Yunbi (CN)

BTC: Poloniex, Bittrex, Liqui

Golen is a coin token, based on Ethereum blockchain technology. Described by some commentators as the "AirBNB of computing", the value of the coin is centered around the software that can be developed using it.

The founders of the Golem Project refer to it as a "supercomputer", with the ability to interconnect with other computers for various purposes. These include scientific research, data analysis and cryptocurrency mining. For example, if your computer has unused power, using the Golem network, you can rent that power (hence the AirBNB comparison) to someone else who needs it. The user who needs the extra power, has the ability to access supercomputer levels of processing power for a fraction of the cost of actually owning the processing power themselves.

The ability for users to earn money for their unused computing power is, in theory, a no-brainer, however what remains to be seen is the practical application of the technology. The Golem team's lack of marketing visibility also appears to hurt the coins value in recent times. The lack of ability to buy GNT using fiat currency (such as USD) is also a drawback for the mass market.

It should be noted that the technology is still very much in the early development stages and as of July 2017, the team are still looking for alpha testers for the project. The Golem Project has a very real possibility of petering out into nothing. On the flip side - there is tremendous potential for large future gains with the price of a coin still under $0.30.

STEEM (STEEM)

Price at time of writing - $1.10

Available on:

Fiat: OpenLedgerDEX (Eur)

BTC: Poloniex, Bittrex

Steem represents one of the more intriguing cryptocurrencies available on the market today. The currency itself is based on the social media platform Steemit. Users can publish content such as blog posts and long form articles, and this content is rewarded in the form of digital currency. Similar to how Reddit users receive upvotes, Steemit users receive Steem tokens known as Steem Dollars. The financial incentive ensures that users strive to produce quality content. The platform allows posts on a multitude of topics ranging from cryptocurrency discussion, to sports news and even poetry.

Steem dollars are worth the equivalent of $1 at the current exchange rate. They must be converted to Steem in order to exchange to fiat currency or other cryptocurrencies. The reasoning behind this is so they can be pegged to the value of the US dollar in order to decrease the risk of inflation devaluing them. Steemit goes further and actually gives users a 10% interest rate on any Steem dollars held in their account for more than a year.

The main drawback is that the success of the coin itself is based on the success of the platform. If the website reaches a plateau in traffic, so will the coin's value. Others have questioned the validity of the site itself, and whether it may be a large scale pump and dump or even a pyramid scheme. The criticism comes from the fact that many of the most upvoted posts were ones that promoted the

Steemit platform itself. Concerns have also been raised with automatic posting bots stealing content in order to gain extra voters.

Creators of the site responded to the criticism by saying that there are certain safeguards in place designed to keep content fresh and give users an extra incentive to hold on to their Steem coins. Their way of doing this is with something known as Steem Power. Steem Power is a way for users to lock up their coins in the long run by directly investing them into the platform itself. By converting Steem to Steem Power, users have a greater weighting of upvotes on the platform and essentially become "power users" for lack of a better term.

One advantage Steem possesses versus other cryptocurrencies is that by design it is the easiest currency to access with zero investment. Instead of simply buying coins on an exchange, or spending money on computer hardware needed to mine coins, users can simply sign up on the website for free and begin posting content in order to gain coins. It represents the lowest barrier to entry for any asset in the cryptocurrency market. Although making significant gains may be tough initially, users have made thousands of dollars worth of Steem from just a single post.

IOTA (MIOTA)

Price at time of writing - $0.92

Available on:

Fiat: Bitfinex

BTC: Bitfinex

IOTA, or the rather uninspiringly named Internet of Things (IOT) Coin, is another coin based on blockchain technology, but with a twist.

The team behind IOTA is basing their hopes on a project known as Tangle, which is a technology currently in development that can be described as a blockchain without blocks. In theory, if Tangle does succeed, an entire network can be decentralized. This would lead to ZERO scalability problems that every other coin faces. To be frank, if the technology does indeed work - it could be a complete game changer for the cryptocurrency scene. In more practical terms, imagine a world without unnecessary middlemen, and think of the sheer cost-saving this would achieve.

The underlying theory behind the coin is near-zero transaction costs, even for transfers of minute amounts of money - something that no other coin or technology promises right now - not even giants like Bitcoin or Ethereum. By focusing on these micro, or nano payments, there are countless uses for both consumer and business based financial technology. The technology is open source, so anyone can see the code behind it, and follow along with the coin's development - if you are so inclined.

The reason for the low price of the coin as it currently stands, is that the technology is right now still firmly theoretical. Issues that plague all cryptocurrency technologies like mass adoption and security will have to be resolved before the coin can take the next step. The development team have many issues to overcome in just the construction of the technology, let alone the marketing.

Dogecoin (DOGE)

Price at time of writing - $0.0019

Available on:

Fiat: YoBit, BTC38 (CN)

BTC: HitBTC, Poloniex, Bittrex

A meme that ended up with actual monetary value. Favored by Shiba Inus worldwide, dogecoin was invented by Jackson Palmer in 2013 and became something of a fad in the cryptocurrency world.

Dogecoin's value largely comes from an internet form of "tipping". The most prominent example of this is holders donating Dogecoin to Reddit users for posts they enjoyed. Dogecoin eventually became the second most "tipped" cryptocurrency after Bitcoin and the market for Dogecoin exploded to a peak of $60million market cap in early 2014. A campaign to send the Jamaican bobsled team to the Winter Olympics was funded in part by the coin and $25,000 worth was donated to a UK service dog charity.

The coin flamed out almost as quickly as it rose after Dogecoin backed exchange Moolah filed for bankruptcy and CEO Ryan Kennedy aka Alex Green/Ryan Gentle was sentenced to 11 years in prison on sexual assault charges. Kennedy was estimated to have caused $2-4million dollars worth of losses for those who funded the project.

The coin's present day status remains that of a lighthearted, fun community based project that rewards forum posts. Dogecoin still possess one of the most active communities of any cryptocurrency and supporters hope that one day the coin will return to its position as one of the internet's most tipped coins.

Exclusive 2018 Bonus Coin

Vertcoin (VTC)

Price at time of publication - $4.32

Available on:

Fiat: LiteBit.eu (EUR), Bittylicious (GBP)

BTC: Poloniex, Bittrex, YoBit

No cryptocurrency has more discussion in Q4 of 2017 than Vertcoin. Just when everyone thought the meteoric altcoin rises of the first half of the year were over, along comes Vertcoin with 600% gains in a little under 6 weeks.

So what makes Vertcoin different from other cryptocurrencies? The answer is in the mining algorithm used.

Vertcoin's mining algorithm is known as "ASIC resistant". ASICs are supercomputers designed for one function (in this case, cryptocurrency mining). ASICs have long been a controversial topic in the mining community, as large computer hardware companies have created these computers and as a result have marginalized those mining on their regular computers at home. This has led to the rise in "mining farms", and concentrated the mining of cryptocurrencies like Bitcoin in the hands of fewer and fewer individuals and organizations.

So how exactly is Vertcoin immune to ASICs? The development team continues to create mining algorithms, the current one known as Lyra2REv2, which favor GPU mining as opposed to CPU mining which ASICs dominate.

The great thing about ASIC resistance from a consumer point of view is that pretty much anyone with a moderately powered computer can mine

Vertcoin without it being a giant drain of resources.

If you want to get started mining Vertcoins you can download their mining software directly onto your PC at http://bit.ly/VertcoinMiner

It also allows 4x faster transactions times than Bitcoin, with a confirmation time of   2.5 minutes versus Bitcoin's 10 minutes.

The coin isn't actually new to the market like some of the others mentioned in this book, it's been around since 2014 - so the development team has already been in for some time, even before the recent jump in price.

No premining, ICOs or airdrops occured, so if you're looking for a comparison, Vertcoin is more similar to Litecoin than it is to say Dash. Another similarity to Litecoin is the fixed supply of 84 million coins.

Vertcoin isn't designed as a replacement for Bitcoin, or even Litecoin, it was made to coexist alongside them. One particular thing to note about Vertcoin going forward is their goal of "atomic swaps", which is the ability to instantly swap Vertcoin for Litecoin or Bitcoin without a transaction fee or cryptocurrency exchange. The platform is currently in its alpha development stage, which successful Vertcoin to Litecoin transactions already processed. If atomic swaps become widely adopted, that can only mean good things for Vertcoin's price, and the cryptocurrency market as a whole going forward.

One thing I particular like about Vertcoin is their development team actively stopping social media posts shilling the coin. It's one thing to point out the benefits of one cryptocurrency, but mindlessly spamming various forums and discussions with rumors of huge gains does nothing to aid legitimate adoption of the technology. If Vertcoin is committed to becoming a serious player in the cryptocurrency market, the less talk of "moons and lambos", the better.

With a halving of mining rewards scheduled for December 12th 2017. This may well be the best time to get involved in the short-term, although continued gains are expected in Q1 of 2018 and beyond - dependent on the success of atomic swaps of course.

Where to store your cryptocurrency - Wallets & Cold Storage

Once you've successfully bought some cryptocurrency, be it Bitcoin, Ethereum or another altcoin, you'll need somewhere to safely store it.

Your cryptocurrency wallet is akin to a regular fiat currency wallet in the sense that you can use it to store and spend money, in addition to seeing exactly how much money you have. However cryptocurrency wallets differ from fiat currency wallets because of the technology behind how the coins are generated. As a reminder, the way the technology works means your cryptocurrency isn't stored in one central location. It is stored within the blockchain. This means there is a public record of ownership for each coin, and when a transaction occurs, the record is updated.

You can store your cryptocurrency on the exchange where you bought it like Coinbase or Poloniex, it is advisable to not do this for a number of reasons.

1. Like any online entity - these exchanges are vulnerable to hacking, no matter how secure they are - or what security measures they take. This happened with the Mt. Gox exchange in June 2011

2. Your passwords to these exchanges are vulnerable to keyloggers, trojan horses and other computer virus type programs

3. You could accidentally authorize a login from a malicious service like coinbose.com (example) instead of coinbase.com

Cold storage refers to any system that takes your cryptocurrency offline. These include offline paper wallets, physical bearer items like physical bitcoin or a USB drive. We will examine the pros and cons of each one.

Cryptocurrency wallets have two keys. A public one, and a private one. These are represented by long character strings. For example, a public key could be 02a1633cafcc01ebfb6d78e39f687a1f0995c62fc95f 51ead10a02ee0be551b5dc[4] - or it could be shown as a QR code. Your public key is the address you use to receive cryptocurrency from others. It is perfectly safe to give your public key to anyone. Those who have access to you public key can only deposit money in your account.

On the other hand, your private key is what enables you to send cryptocurrency to others. For

---

[4] This is not a real wallet address, do not send money to it

every transaction, the recipient's public key, and the sender's private key are used.

It is advisable to have an offline backup of your private key in case of hardware failure, or data theft. If anyone has access to your private key, they can withdraw funds from your account, which leads us to the number one rule of cryptocurrency storage.

The number one rule of Cryptocurrency storage: Never give anyone your private key. Ever.

Paper Wallets:

Paper wallets are simply notes of your private key that are written down on paper. They will often feature QR codes so the sender can quickly scan them to send cryptocurrency.

Pros:

- Cheap

- Your private keys are not stored digitally, and are therefore not subject to cyber-attacks or hardware failures.

Cons:

- Loss of paper due to human error

- Paper is fragile and can degrade quickly in certain environments

- Not easy to spend cryptocurrency quickly if necessary - not useful for everyday transactions

Recommendations:

It is recommended you store your paper wallet in a sealed plastic bag to protect against water or damp conditions. If you are holding cryptocurrency for the long-term, store the paper inside a safe.

Ensure you read and understand the step-by-step instructions before printing any paper wallets.

Bitcoin:

http://bitaddress.org

http://bitcoinpaperwallet.com

Ethereum:

http://myetherwallet.com/

Litecoin:

https://liteaddress.org/

For all other currencies - consult a reputable cryptocurrency forum for the latest recommendations on paper and offline storage wallets.

Hardware Wallets

Hardware wallet refer to physical storage items that contain your private key. The most common form of these are encrypted USB sticks.

These wallets use two factor authentication or 2FA to ensure that only the wallet owner can access the data. For example, one factor is the physical USB stick plugged into your computer, and the other would be a 4 digit pin code - much like how you use a debit card to withdraw money from an ATM.

Pros:

● Near impossible to hack - as of the time of writing, there have been ZERO instances of hacked hardware wallets

● Even if your computer is infected with a virus or malware, the wallet cannot be accessed due to 2FA

- The private key never leaves your device or transfers to a computer, so once again, malware or infected computers are not an issue

- Can be carried with you easily if you need to spend your cryptocurrency

- Transactions are easier than with paper wallets

- Can store multiple addresses on one device

- For the gadget lovers among you - they look a lot cooler than a folded piece of paper

Cons:

- More expensive than paper wallets - starting at around $60

- Susceptible to hardware damage, degradation and changes in technology

- Different wallets support different cryptocurrencies

- Trusting the provider to deliver an unused wallet. Using a second hand wallet is a big security breach. Only purchase hardware wallets from official sources.

The most popular of these are the Trezor and Ledger wallets. For altcoins that are not supported by these wallet, you can create your own encrypted USB wallet by following online tutorials.

Cryptocurrency Investing Mindset

FOMO & FUD - 2 Terms to be Cautious of

In cryptocurrency terms, FOMO and FUD are two of the most potentially dangerous words in an investor's lexicon. No, they aren't the latest hotshot coins coming out of China, they are acronyms that have cost naive traders and investors money.

FOMO - Fear Of Missing Out

Fear of missing out causes people to over invest and throw money at coins without proper research or due diligence. If you spend any time on cryptocurrency forums, you will see hundreds of posts from those new to the market asking for tips on which coins to buy. It seems like every day there is a new shiny object that people are hyping up, causing less experienced investors to blindly throw their money at it. This leads to people buying coins at their peak, and then panic selling them when the coin pulls back a few days later.

The important thing to remember is this, you won't be able to win on every investment you make. You won't be able to buy every single coin at the right time, and people will make money where you cannot. The important thing is to only measure yourself against yourself, and take stock of your own profit/loss sheet. Before you invest in a coin, take a second to ask yourself why you are choosing to do so, and re-examine the fundamentals of the coin itself.

Anxiety caused by potentially missing out on huge returns is only natural, and something that nearly all of us suffer from. The best way to combat this is to understand blockchain technology, and to research each coin individually before deciding to invest. By making smart, reasoned investments, you have a much better chance of long term profits.

FUD - Fear, Uncertainty and Doubt

Fear, uncertainty and doubt is information to dissuade investors from believing in cryptocurrencies and their applications. This can be anything from spreading of misinformation (such as the fake Vitalik Buterin death rumors), to news reports discounting real world usage of cryptocurrency technology.

Certain nefarious cryptocurrency figures have used FUD to push their own agenda while attempting to harm the growth of other coins. This is where it is important to differentiate from reasonable criticism and analysis of a coin vs. FUD. The more informed you are, the easier it is for you to see the difference.

Where you are getting your news from is another factor. Social media is the king of FUD, go to any crypto group on Facebook or watch a YouTube video from one of the larger channels and you will see commentors spreading FUD on every video. Instead, focus on larger crypto news websites where FUD is less prevalent, and remember to consume your news from more than one source.

Short term gain vs. Long term investment

Billionaire hedge fund manager and cryptocurrency investor Michael Novogratz made a very good analogy when he compared the current state of the market to the third inning of a baseball game. The market is still very much developing, and there are a number of short and long term events that can effect the price of currencies.

Unlike regular stock market, the cryptocurrency market is running 24/7 365 - there are no delays between information coming to light and the market reacting, there is no dead time.

If you believe in the technology behind the currencies, then these coins absolutely make sense as a long term investment. With many coins, time in the market beats timing the market, which is where our next acronym comes from.

HODL: Hold On (For) Dear Life

A backronym that is a play on "hold" - it focuses on holding on to your coins even when the market is dropping.

A more lighthearted explanation comes from Bitcointalk forum poster "GameKyuubi" who inadvertently invented the term in 2013 while inebriated (author's note: Do not trade or purchase cryptocurrency under the influence)

"WHY AM I HOLDING? I'LL TELL YOU WHY. It's because I'm a bad trader and I KNOW I'M A BAD TRADER.
I SHOULD HAVE SOLD MOMENTS BEFORE EVERY SELL AND BOUGHT MOMENTS

BEFORE EVERY BUY BUT YOU KNOW WHAT NOT EVERYBODY IS AS COOL AS YOU."

With any long term investment, you are going to see market downturns - that's simply how capitalism works. If you panic and sell every time you see a slight dip (and with cryptocurrencies, that's going to happen A LOT), then you've got a surefire way to lose money in the long run.

HODL'ing of course has its potential downsides as well, with more and more coins coming to market - it's obvious that not all of them will continue to go up in price. You can compare it to the regular stock market with blue chip stocks and penny stocks. Just because a penny stock or small market cap cryptocurrency is currently trading for $0.08, does not mean it has the right to rise indefinitely. If the company or people behind the cryptocurrency don't fulfill their promises to the market, then the coin's value will crash and it will eventually become obsolete.

Remember - hindsight is easy. Timing market movements in a market as volatile as cryptocurrencies on the other hand, is not. Approach each investment with caution, and proper research.

Paper profits vs. Actual profits

Remember, until you have sold your coins, any profit you have made is strictly on paper. With the cryptocurrency market being as volatile as it is, profit margins drastically shift and can do so on a daily, or even an hourly basis. That is why I recommend taking intermediate profits for yourself when investing, you do this by sell a proportion of your holdings at a profit.

For example, you buy 1 coin at $100, 1 month later the coin's value has risen to $150. If you trade out $75 worth of the coin at $150, then you still have 0.5 coins worth $75 on paper and an extra $75 in cold, hard cash. Taking money for yourself is a smart play, and something you should absolutely do if you are looking to make consistent profits over time.

The inverse rule of this is to not sell on the dip. If you followed rule number one of investing which was to not invest more than you could afford to lose, you have zero reason to sell at a loss. Yes, you may see scary headlines with "Ethereum drops 40%" or "Litecoin is crashing", but in the long-run, the majority of these coins return to their previous, and even higher levels. If you sell at a loss, then your money is gone forever.

The Chaincoin Pump and Dump Scheme - Why You Should Always Research a Coin Before Buying

The following is a lesson in smart investing, and who you get your information from.

Chaincoin (CHC) was a cryptocurrency that underwent a meteoric prise rise from $0.05 to over $6 in under a week. Prior to this, the coin was only available on two small cryptocurrency exchanges and had very little total trading volume. The official Github (programming community) and Twitter accounts had been dead for months prior to this, and very few technical milestones had been accomplished.

Despite this, a YouTube channel known as HighOnCoins started heavily promoting the coin. Videos titled "Buy ChainCoin $CHC" appeared on the channel. The channel also encouraged users to set up masternodes (which required 1000 CHC). The channel encouraged people to buy and hold indefinitely rather than trading out for a profit. The underlying theory behind this was that if everyone invested and held the coin, then the price would continue to increase and grow.

However Chaincoin suffered from many fundamental flaws including:

- Lack of differentiation from other coins
- Lack of innovation from developers
- Zero real world applications versus other coins

The initial surge in investing caused a stir in the cryptocurrency community. Mixed reactions ranging from confusion from investors focused on coin fundamentals, to excitement from uninformed players who believed they were about to get rich quick.

The coin reached an all time high of $6.81 on July 14th 2017, a few days later, developers returned to the coin's GitHub page and made a couple of superficial changes. Within 5 days the price of the coin crashed back to $1. HighOnCoins claimed this was as a result of hackers, although exchange activity showed a large dumping of coins from a few traders.

Chaincoin currently trades at $0.32.

GitHub blog Store of Value summarized the incident with the following statement "This was a blatant transfer of wealth from the foolish to the nefarious." Let this be a lesson, never invest in a coin based on hype. Instead, do so on fundamentals and belief in the technology.

Conclusion

I hope you have learned many things about cryptocurrency and how you can profit from investing or trading in these coins. There are various factors to consider when investing in coins and you can use these to decide on an investing or trading strategy.

You may want to read this material one or two more times, and make some choices as to what your goals are for your relationship with the cryptocurrency market.

Next, decide how you will go about reaching those goals. Decide on a cryptocurrency exchange and how you will store your assets BEFORE investing in any one or more coins.

Then plan out how much you will invest in each coin. Remember, diversity is important and you should never have all of your long-term holdings in a single coin.

If you are going to buy cryptocurrencies, do so using Dollar cost averaging – this means that you don't buy all of your coins in one trade but instead buy a fixed amount every month, week or even day throughout the year. This allows you to not be tied to a single price and instead average out your investments so they are less exposed to volatile price movements.

Trade rationally, not emotionally. If you plan on holding coins for the long-term, do not check charts every few hours, or you will drive yourself crazy. Things change quickly in this market so stay informed on cryptocurrency news and happenings, you can do this in less than 30 minutes per day.

Ensure you consume information from a variety of non-biased sources.

And never invest in a coin because "some guy on the internet" told you to.

Finally, if you found this book useful, I would greatly appreciate it if you would review this book on Amazon.

Thank you for reading, I hope you make A LOT of money in the cryptocurrency market.

P.S.

If you sign up for Coinbase using this link, you will receive $10 worth of FREE BITCOIN after your first purchase of more than $100 worth of any cryptocurrency.

http://bit.ly/10dollarbtc

Blockchain Beginners Bible:

Discover How Blockchain Could Enrich Your Life, Your Business & Your Cryptocurrency Wallet

By Stephen Satoshi

Introduction

Hi, I'm Stephen and I'm a blockchain addict.

Well, enthusiast is probably a better term - although I still definitely check my cryptocurrency portfolio far too frequently.

I've certainly come a long way from the young man who first heard about this Bitcoin thing back in the 2010s. You know, that new internet currency that people were making money from.

How could a currency be worth anything if it isn't backed by a central government? Oh, how naive I was.

This initial exposure to Bitcoin sparked an interest in blockchain technology and it's potential. I try to refrain from hyperbole but I truly believe this is mankind's greatest invention since Tim Berners-Lee invented the world wide web back in 1989.

You see, although Bitcoin and cryptocurrency in general is a large part of the blockchain movement, it goes beyond that.

There are serious political, social and economic ramifications that will come as a result of decentralization. An incorruptible permanent record, accessible by the masses, has a myriad of uses that can undoubtedly benefit society as a whole.

If you're reading this book, you're mostly likely a skeptic of big government, and you have every right to be. As recently as 2016, we witnessed a United States General Election in which both sides accused the other of vote tampering, in what is supposedly the world's leading democracy.

In short, governance as we know it has to be questioned.

Blockchain technology allows for indisputable trust on a level such as this. Banks, governments, hospitals, all the way down to small one-man-operation businesses can benefit.

That is the true future of this technology.

I hope this is just the start of your blockchain journey, and I hope it not only makes you a lot of money, I hope it enriches the quality of your life.

One final thing, if you enjoy this book I'd appreciate it if you took 2 minutes to leave it a review on Amazon.

Thanks,

Stephen

Chapter 1: What is Blockchain Technology?

Over the past few years, you have likely heard more and more people talking about cryptocurrency this, or blockchain that. If you don't understand these terms, don't worry, you aren't alone. It may be time to jump on the bandwagon, however, as blockchain use is rapidly approaching consumer status with IBM estimating that 15 percent of banks will already be using blockchain technology by the end of 2017.

Simply put, blockchain is the foundation that makes technologies like cryptocurrency possible. On a fundamental level, a blockchain takes data, primarily of financial nature for now, and replicates that data across a vast number of decentralized nodes that could conceivably be spread around the entire world. This process is run not by a centralized network or body, but by a peer-to-peer approach that uses cryptography and digital signatures to keep things running smoothly.

Each new block in a chain contains information regarding various transactions, and possibly what are known as smart contracts, as well as information that links it to the blocks around it. Each block is also timestamped which helps the chain determine its place in the whole thing. The transactions in individual blocks are verified by block miners, third parties who are paid for their work, and are only then added to the chain as a whole.

What miners are actually doing is solving what are known as proof-of-work systems which means they are solving complicated mathematical equations using specialized equipment designed for doing so. The equations prevent security breaches through denial of service attacks and keep things running smoothly. The amount of reward for this type of work varies based on the cryptocurrency that is being mined, as well as the number of people working to complete the block they were chosen to mine. Most cryptocurrencies also charge a small transaction fee, and a part of that fee goes to the miners as well.

Despite the fact that the database information is spread around the world with no central authority, and the fact that sections of it are inspected by third parties on a regular basis, the data that is stored in a blockchain remains incredibly secure. This level of security doesn't come from an active offense against fraud, it comes from the defensive capabilities of the way in which the blockchain is constructed.

If a specific transaction that is being transferred from a node doesn't match up with what the other nodes are saying then that block is discarded in favor of a more accurate one. Essentially, for a false block to make it past the blockchain's defenses, it would need to show up on 51 percent of all of the nodes in the system at the same time.

The difficulty of such a task means that it could be done, but the costs involved would more than outweigh the potential reward for doing so.

History lesson

In order to understand the true importance of blockchain technology, it is helpful to understand a little bit about its history. In 2008, a person or a group of persons using the alias Satoshi Nakamoto put forth a whitepaper on the idea of a digital currency that would allow individuals to transfer money to one another in a largely anonymous fashion. This paper, titled, *bitcoin: A Peer-to Peer Electronic Cash System,* was soon followed by the original blockchain and bitcoin code from the same alias. The code was released in an open source fashion, and the Nakamoto name faded from sight as other developers began working on the code in earnest.

The Nakamoto alias was also the first person to distribute bitcoins and then verify the transaction, receiving 50 bitcoins for doing so. For those who are considering investing in a cryptocurrency based on blockchain technology, take note, as the first use of those bitcoins was to trade 10,000 of them for a pair of large pizzas which made each worth about $.002. If you weren't aware, they are doing a little better than that these days with each bitcoin being worth nearly $5,000 as of September 2017.

By 2014, blockchain usage was gaining some traction and a new and improved version of the original code now allowed for entire programs to be contained in blocks along with data that make it possible for a wide variety of tasks to be carried out from within the blockchain. In 2016, the Russian Federation started working on a blockchain program as a means of collecting royalties for copyrighted material, making Russia the first country to official announce a blockchain project, though since that time a number of other countries, including China and the US, have indicated they are working on blockchain projects of their own. When the project was announced, the Russian Economic Minister was quoted as saying that blockchain technology was likely the most important new technology since the invention of the internet.

Over the past few years, another blockchain based company, the Ethereum platform has been gaining a lot of support due to its wide variety of enhanced capabilities when compared to the bitcoin blockchain. The Ethereum platform has its own official cryptocurrency, ether (although the two terms are used interchanably by many commentators), and is also home to an ecosystem of other cryptocurrencies that other programmers have made to run in its framework. It is also home to a wide variety of smart contracts and apps that run on "gas", which is essentially a transaction fee the platform collects for each transaction. Ether blocks that are mind tend to be completed in a shorter timeframe than bitcoin blocks and the Ethereum chain can handle a great many more blocks at a time when compared to the bitcoin chain.

Database differences: The biggest difference between a blockchain database and a traditional database is the level of centralization that is required in order for it to run effectively. Even if a traditional server is decentralized, the core components are going to be arranged as close to one another as possible to facilitate the transfer of information. Instead, blockchains are formed of nodes that are separated by thousands of miles, each communicating with the others through a best use model that means they naturally seek out the nodes that are closest to them and the information spreads out from there.

The fact that mass collaboration and the blockchain code results in a reliable means by which funds can be transferred is a game changer. Blockchain is the first innately digital medium where value can be transferred, in much the way the internet allowed for information to be transmitted digitally.

Hashes: A hash is a mathematical function that makes up a crucial part of the blockchain security matrix. This is the function that ensures the data that is added to a blockchain remains secure regardless of who might get their hands on it. The function encrypts the data in such a way that it becomes a fixed length output, which can be thought of as a type of digital fingerprint. When it comes to blockchain security the most commonly used hash function is SHA-256. SHA-256 is used by cryptocurrencies such as Bitcoin, Omni and Zetacoin.

The hash function for every block is going to be different, which means that if that data is altered by a malevolent third party then the entire fingerprint would be rearranged in unpredictable ways. Additional hash information is added once the block is added to the chain as a whole. This process is repeated throughout the blockchain each time a new block is added so that it is always changing.

Merkle trees: Hashes are then used by a process known as the Merkle tree which is a quick and easy way for the blockchain to verify all of its data once a new block has been added. Each hash is unique and created based on the data it contains which means the Merkle tree then essentially needs to scan the hash, compare it to the root hashes which is the ultimate collection of all the hashes, and then determine if everything lines up as it should. Each time it does this, it creates a pair of roots, one where the data is correct and one where it is not, this way it keeps the core details of the blockchain intact against malicious changes.

Chapter 2: Practical Application of Blockchain Technology

As blockchain technology continues to grow in popularity, the ways in which it can be put to use are growing as well. What follows are a number of different ways blockchain technology is sure to change how business is conducted, day to day life, outside the realm of cryptocurrency and how governments and lawmakers interact with the public.

Business uses

Money transfers and payments: While blockchain technology is already synonymous with cryptocurrency payments, the fact of the matter is that more can be done in that space to facilitate the needs of businesses when it comes to utilizing blockchain to its fullest potential. The Ethereum Enterprise Alliance is a group of major corporations such as Microsoft, JP Morgan and Samsung that are working together to build a blockchain that is based on Ethereum technology but also contains the level of control that businesses would need in order to use the technology on a regular basis.

This type of service, while extremely common in some parts of the world, are extremely hard to come by in others. As such, more people in Kenya currently have a bitcoin wallet than have indoor plumbing. Connecting all these new individuals to the internet is going to have serious positive ramifications for retailers worldwide.

Notary services: Blockchain technology is constructed in such a way that it could conceivably be used to replace traditional notary services. There are already numerous different apps available that allow for notarization of a variety of different types of content.

Cloud storage: Blockchain technology is already being used as a means of connecting users with cloud storage space in an Airbnb like setup. Using this system those with spare storage space on their hard drives can rent out the extra space to those who are in need of extra storage. The estimate is that worldwide spending has reached more than $20 billion for cloud storage so this could be a profitable opportunity if this catches on.

Fraud: Blockchain technology has the potential to increase the efficacy of tracking identities online in a way that is both efficient and secure. Blockchain is uniquely situated to solve this problem because its results are sure to be properly authenticated, immutable, secure and irrefutable. This improved system will do away with complicated password or dual factor authentication systems in favor of a system that will ultimately use digital signatures and cryptography to keep everyone safe and efficiently catalogued.

Using this type of system, the transaction will be processed as normal, and the only check that will be required is if the account from which the funds are drawn, matches the account of the person who authorized the transaction. A variation of this same usage of the technology can also be used when it comes to birth certificates, passports, residency forms, account logins and physical identification. There are already apps available that utilize a blockchain to verify the identity of users from a mobile device.

Supply chain communication: If it is one thing that companies have a hard time dealing with, it is the extreme level of communication that is required in order to ensure that they have all the requirements at the ready to ensure they are ready to do whatever it is they do. Blockchain technology allows for companies to easily track products from door to door, with the internet of things (the ability for everyday objects to send and receive data) connecting shipping containers to accounts that get a steady stream of details about the product in question as it crosses various thresholds and ultimately automatically pays for the goods once they have reached their final location. SkuChain and Provenance are two companies that are working to create these types of systems.

Gift cards: Gift cards are a good idea in theory that ultimately falls apart in practice when it comes time for the customer to actually hold onto the card in question. Blockchain technology has the potential to change all that by connecting customer loyalty products directly to a blockchain which can then verify and update relevant information as needed. Gyft Block is a company that already has a digital gift card up and running on the bitcoin blockchain that can be traded just like a cryptocurrency.

Internet of things: Samsung and IBM are currently working together on a concept referred to as the Autonomous Decentralized Peer-to-Peer Telemetry or ADEPT, which uses blockchain as a means of creating a system that mixes proof of stake and proof of work systems to better secure transactions. Essentially, what they are trying to do is to create a blockchain that would act like a public ledger for a wide number of devices. This public ledger would then serve as a hub which can create a bridge between devices for a very low cost. These devices could then communicate with one another in a practically autonomous fashion, making it easy to save energy, sort out bugs and issue updates.

Insurance contracts: Smart contracts have the possibility to reinvent insurance in a big way.

Rather than deal with insurance agents who have to determine liability in case of a business-related injury, a blockchain would be able to make use of a smart contract that issues payments if a specific interconnected item registers a faulty signal. Blockchain would then allow for a more streamlined claim process that would improve the customer experience and ultimately save the company money.

Funding: 4G Capital is a company that provides access to credit for small businesses in Africa through the use of a decentralized app that is running off of the Ethereum blockchain. Donors are able to use the app to spend their cryptocurrency funds directly to the recipient of their choice. The money is then converted to the currency of the applicant and dispersed using a proprietary transaction system. In addition to providing 100 percent unsecured loans to those who often would not be able to get them otherwise, it also provides business training and consulting services. While currently operating in a limited capacity, if it proves successful more operations offering this type of funding are sure to appear.

Microblogging: Businesses are always looking for new ways to interact with their target audience and blockchain may be the next new frontier. Projects like Eth-Tweet offer decentralized microblogging services through the Ethereum blockchain. The service operates much like Twitter, except that as a truly decentralized entity there is no one who can pressure users to take content down and no one can remove messages after they have been added to the chain.

Day to Day Life

Healthcare: Real world tests are already being done that link individuals to their healthcare status as they are going through a hospital. Early studies from the MIT Media Lab show that this practice can decrease errors by up to 30 percent in nonemergency situations. This is a huge step forward for hospitals that are often not designed for the volume and range of data that is being created these days. Patient data can even continue to be gathered on an outpatient basis or if the individual has agreed to be part of a test group. Payment for these tests could then be issued automatically once the required data has been successfully gathered.

Internet decentralization: With the rise of Google, the internet is a much more centralized place than it once was. A startup by the name of Blockstack is working to change all of that. It is on track to release prototype software in the second half of

2017 which will make it possible for anyone to utilize blockchain technology to access a version of the internet where you have much more control over your personal data. This decentralized internet will act the same way the traditional internet does, except that instead of creating a different account for every website, the process will reverse and you will create a primary account, then give certain sites access to it.

If you are then finished using a specific site you can then completely revoke its access to your data at any time. While this might seem like a small step, it is actually a giant leap for a new and improved internet. Blockstack makes use of a digital ledger to track usernames and various levels of encryption, with the end result being a greater degree of privacy control for the individual user. The blockchain will also keep track of domain names as well, potentially making ICANN, the web domain oversight body, obsolete. Microsoft is already in talks with Blockstack to make use of its technology.

While the way it handles web functions might seem extreme, it is actually the low-level features of the internet as a whole that have led to the dominance of corporations who essentially have free reign to treat user data as they see fit. The new platform will still offer companies ways to make money while providing services, the balance of power is just going to favor the consumer more than it does now.

Improved property rights: Both tangible and intangible property from cars and houses on one hand to company shares and patents on the other, can all be connected via smart contract and blockchain technology to make determining the rights to these items much less complicated than it currently is. These details could be stored in a type of decentralized ledger along with related contractual details regarding the true ownership of the property in question. The technology could even extend to smart keys which could then give specific users access to specific property.

The ledger would keep track of the finer details and activate specific keys as needed. In this case the decentralized ledger is also a system for managing and recording property rights and also creating duplicates if smart keys are lost. Implementing smart property protocols will help to decrease the average property owner's risk of fraud, questionable business deals and mediation fees.

New types of money lenders: With blockchain technology making it easier and easier to transfer funds between individuals, new types of hard money lenders are already popping up to take advantage of the fact. Hard money lenders are more likely to offer terms to individuals who already have subpar credit, unfortunately the terms are often quite high and often property is listed as collateral. This, in turn, causes many debtors to default on loans, and leaves them in a worse position than they were in initially. Lending via blockchain technology has the potential to change all of that as the binding nature of the transaction means that less collateral will be required and smart contracts can take care of the transactions themselves so costs will be decreased as well.

Smarter smartphones: Smartphones already operate on a type of cryptography in that they require either your fingerprint, a scan of your face, or a password in order to activate them. This is already a form of smart property, just in its nascent stages. This facet of personal technology will be enhanced via blockchain technology in that, rather than having these details tied to your physical SIM card, they will be stored in the blockchain where you can easily access them no matter where you are. While issues concerning security would typically arise in these sorts of situations, the fact that each transaction needs to be verified in order to add it to the chain ensures security remains tight.

Passports: Blockchains have been helping people manage their passports since at least 2014 by making it easier for users to identify themselves regardless if they are online or offline. This system works by taking a picture of the user and encoding it with a private key as well as a public one. The passport is then stored in a public ledger which can be accessed via a blockchain address by the person who has the key.

Important documents: It doesn't matter if it is a wedding certificate, birth certificate or death certificate, all of these documents confer various rights or privileges. This would be less of an issue if it weren't for the fact that the physical systems that keep track of these details are prone to mistakes. In fact, according to UNICEF, as many as 30 percent of all children who are below the age of five do not have a birth certificate. Implementing a public blockchain to streamline this process would not only make keeping track of these services more manageable, it will make these documents easier to obtain as well.

Identification: Currently you have to carry your driver's license, your work identification card, your social security card, the list goes on and on. With the right blockchain, however, all of this could be a thing of the past. Eventually everyone is going to have a digital ID that goes with them everywhere. It will be connected to a worldwide protected ledger and it will contain all the basic details you now need to carry around with you.

Improve digital interactions: With a wider and wider variety of interactions being initiated online, it is often difficult to know whom you can trust. Blockchain can alleviate that problem by storing a version of your identity in a blockchain that is available for everyone to see. It would automatically pull in things like review scores and rankings from a wide variety of sites so you always have at least a general idea of what you are in for before taking an online interaction into the real world. Unlike with more traditional types of social media, users would not have the ability to remove their information and start fresh, once it is in the blockchain it would be there forever.

Change the way you fuel your vehicle: Modern electric vehicles have already made great strides when it comes to the fueling process. Another important stride is on the horizon and it has to do with blockchain. Soon blockchain technology will be able to track the electricity that a given owner uses and automatically deduct the funds from the relevant account. All the owner would need to do is pull up to the charging station, the blockchain will take care of the rest.

Beyond Cryptocurrency

Fund HIV research: The UBS bank recently donated a platform to Finclusion systems that will launch a smart contract called HealBond which will seek out efficient trades on the bonds market so that the funds that it makes can ultimately be put to use for HIV research. Analysts are confident that with the right level of passive strategy it could start making money right away. If this proves successful then it will give those with the resources to do so even more ways to help out their favorite causes.

Data security: The company Factom is turning its focus to properly securing data. Currently it is working with the country of Honduras to more accurately register land and also with a number of cities in China on what are known as Smart Cities. Blockchain technology is looking to an integral tool in getting all the various different systems communicating with one another on the same level.

This includes things like data notarization services as well as information management with a much higher level of integrity than what is currently available to the public. Factom has also already received funding from the US Department of Homeland Security, specifically the Technology and Science Directorate to work on the Blockchain Software to Prove Integrity of Captured Data project.

Decentralize the power grid: Rather than requiring a centralized power provider that is in charge of sending energy to workplaces and homes, a decentralized blockchain could be built to allow people to generate power through solar and other means and then sell what they don't need on an open market. All of these transactions would then be visible on the blockchain, keeping fraud to a minimum. As more and more individuals are purchasing high-capacity batteries along with solar panels for their rooftops, this type of scenario is fast becoming a realistic possibility.

Track things that are difficult to track: The fact that a blockchain can show up at any time and cannot be altered makes it uniquely qualified to track the types of items that always seem to go missing. For example, the company Everledger is currently working on a way to identify specific objects and then determine whether or not they are legitimate. So far, they have created a distributed ledger that follows various diamond transaction verifications including law enforcement agencies, claimants, insurance companies and owners to put together a mine to store view of each diamond. The system is useful in that it keeps the supply chain honest and also makes it easier for individual buyers to determine if a given diamond is right for them. Furthermore, smart contracts make it possible for the diamond transactions to clearly be paid for while also tracking them, guaranteeing to consumers that they are not purchasing blood diamonds.

Getting artists what they deserve: Rather than having to worry about making sure their music isn't used without generating compensation, with blockchain, musicians will soon be able to determine who used each song and for what, with each individual transaction being carried out via smart contracts through a blockchain platform. What's more, rather than having to wait for funds to hit a specific level, or for someone, somewhere, to cut a check, these funds would be distributed in relatively real time. This same process can be applied to music licensing as a whole which means it will eventually be possible to cut out middlemen from the equation entirely. This, in turn, means a decrease in costs to the consumer and an increase in profit for the musicians as it means people are more likely to pay for content again.

Improved communication: Currently if your vehicle receives a safety recall then the maker of the vehicle sends out a notice to all of its licensed sales outlets and each of these outlets then reaches out to its customers who have purchased the vehicle in question. This information then may or may not reach you, allowing you to then make an informed decision based on the details you have available to you. The recall could be for something major, or something inconsequential, but regardless you are certainly going to want to know about it. Placing all of this information onto a blockchain would dramatically simplify the process as after the defect was found, the chain could automatically notify the owners in question.

Clarifying asset lifecycles: It doesn't matter who you are or what you do, you have certain tools that make your life possible. Blockchain technology has the ability to make sure you know as much about them as you need to when combined with the internet of things. Asset lifecycle is important for everyone from home business owners to multinational corporations, and the information provided by this type of blockchain could literally save lives. For example, think about an airplane which is likely to have several different owners during its time in the air. This type of blockchain would make it possible for every owner to understand every part on their airplane more completely and to ensure that proper maintenance has been completed throughout its lifetime.

Tracking the food chain: An increase in the ready availability of blockchain technology means that slowly but surely concerns about the quality of the food that you consume on a regular basis will be put to rest. Regardless of the final state of the product when you purchase it, you should be able to see the entire route it took to get to your table. Not just the completed product either, everything that went into the construction of the completed whole. This is particularly useful as there may be more to the traditional food chain than you might first realize. For example, a farm could produce vegetables that head to a processing facility before ending up in a distribution center before being purchased and run through another processing facility, all to end up in a can of tomato soup.

Change the value of ownership: The company Slock.it is based on the Ethereum platform and runs a blockchain for what is known as the

Universal Share Network, this network is an opensource marketplace where anyone can go to list their unused asset, regardless if it is machinery, shipping containers, office space and more. It is a sort of automated AirBnB that works for anything and everything, not just temporary living arrangements. The fundamentals of blockchain technology are then passed on to tangible, real world assets.

Transportation: A variation in the trend towards the crowdsourcing of ridesharing applications, La'Zooz is a decentralized transportation platform that is owned by its users who use blockchain technology to organize and optimize a variety of smart transportation solutions.

Government and lawmakers

Everywhere around the world, government organizations are rapidly exploring the many possibilities provided by blockchain and distributed ledger technology. The ability to suddenly be able to record and distribute ledger information easily and securely has created a market for a variety of new governmental approaches when it comes to establishing trust, preventing fraud and improving transparency.

From a recent survey from the Economic Intelligence Unit as well as IBM, it is clear that the interest in blockchain technology from various worldwide governments is quite high. In fact, as many as 9 out of 10 government agencies are already planning on investing in blockchain based contract management, asset management, regulatory compliance and transaction management by 2018. Meanwhile 7 of the 10 predict blockchain is going to significantly change the way that contract management is handled. Finally, nearly 20 percent say that they expect to have a blockchain plan up and running before the end of 2017.

Voting: As recently as the 2016 United States general election, both Republicans and Democrats could be heard questioning the security of the existing voting system. Likewise, the 2000 presidential election proved that the way that votes are tallied is remarkably out of date. While concerns about hacking have limited the acceptance of electronic means of voting so far, blockchain technology could easily put those fears to rest. A decentralized public ledger would naturally be encrypted but specific individuals could still confirm their votes were counted accurately. This system would not only be more efficient, but it would be more cost effective, and clearly more secure as well.

Responsive, open data: The blockchain ledger would also create a platform for what is known as responsive, open data. Studies show that this type of freely accessible data is likely to bring in nearly $3 trillion worldwide within the first year. Startups will be able to utilize this data to help get ahead of fraudulent activity, parents would be able to access details about the medications their children are receiving, the list is literally endless. Currently, this type of data is only available via limited, government approved windows which are not designed to put citizens first. As a blockchain is a type of public ledger, citizens would be able to access its data at any time and place.

Self-management: Blockchain provides the opportunity for governmental agencies to self-manage more easily as the exchange of information on a global scale would be greatly improved overall. There would be a great deal more trust as well because the information in the blockchain would be public for everyone to see.

Reducing administration costs: If property records were recorded to a blockchain then prospective buyers could more easily, quickly and cost effectively verify ownership information. This process is currently still done manually which means government agencies spend hundreds of thousands of dollars per year paying individuals who do this type of job. Manually verifying such things can also lead to an increased number of errors which helps to further increase potential costs.

It would also greatly decrease the amount of manual effort which would be required on the banks' end as they would have to do much less work when it comes to title insurance. Title insurance is required by lenders as a means to protect their interests. This, in turn, would decrease prices for homebuyers who are refinancing or buying for the first time because they would have to pay less throughout the entire process as the amount of labor would be reduced significantly.

Decrease money laundering: If identity data was readily store on a blockchain, the government agencies could more easily keep track of those who are moving large amounts of money from one place to another. Financial organizations could scan the details of every new client and that information could then be passed along to appropriate agencies if a need presented itself. Furthermore, storing payment and account information in a blockchain would go a long way to standardize the type of information required for an account. This, in turn, will help to improve the quality of the data that is gathered and reduce the number of legitimate transactions that are falsely listed as fraudulent. Finally, having a record that was known to be tamper-proof would make it easier for these organizations to comply with AML regulations.

Ensuring taxpayers are paying up: The Federal Government is likely already working on its own form of cryptocurrency, so there is no reason to assume they are not already working on a means of linking a blockchain to the current IRS system. This blockchain would not only record the amount of money each citizen earned in a year but also any incentives, subsidies, grants and loans that individual might have been provided with as well as there original source. While this will likely lead to more individuals having to pay more in taxes than they are currently, it will also keep the government accountable for every dime that they bring in. It will be much more difficult for money to disappear into the folds of bureaucratic pockets when a blockchain that anyone can see is keeping track of the tab.

Keeping track of incorporated company details:
The state of Delaware marks the first state in the
nation offer incorporated businesses the ability to
keep track of their shareholder rights as well as
their equity via blockchain. As it is common for
many companies to incorporate in Delaware to
take advantage of friendly taxation privileges, this
has the potential to be a change that has
wide-ranging results. The state is also moving its
archival records onto a distributed ledger, so that
more people can view it, for free, at less cost to
taxpayers.

Digital proof of residency: In Estonia, long known
for its forward-thinking practices, it is now
possible to digitally apply for residency in the
country through the use of a governmental
blockchain. New residents then receive a digital
key card that corresponds to a cryptographic key
that can be used to sign secure documents, taking
the place of any signatures on official paperwork.
Virtual residents are then free to open up bank
accounts in Estonia's online banking system,

183

which also utilizes blockchain, as well as incorporate a company or access other e-services. Estonia is proud to be pushing the boundaries of digital transactions and seeing a variety of new monetary streams in the process.

Welfare: In the United Kingdom, blockchain has already been turned into a service that is available to purchase through the Digital Marketplace run by the government. Through this service, various governmental agencies freely experiment, deploy and build digital services based on blockchain and technology based on distributed ledgers. Last year they ran a trial through the Department for Work and Pension that allowed users to take advantage of a mobile app that let them access their monthly benefit payments along with transferring details to a separate distributed ledger as a means of helping them with managing their finances, with their consent of course.

Global Blockchain Council: The Global Blockchain Council has been set up in Dubai and represents more than 50 public and private organizations that have already launched proof-of-concept blockchain projects across the shipping, tourism, digital wills, business registration, title transfer, healthcare records and diamond trading sectors. IBM has also partnered with the organization in hopes of using its blockchain for a logistics and trade solution. The government of Dubai has also announced plans for an initiative to transfer all of their government documents onto an interconnected blockchain by 2020. The estimated cost reduction from this program is anticipated to be at 25.1 million-man hours per year.

The future of blockchain

While blockchain technology is still in a nascent enough stage that virtually anything can happen, there are a number of things that are being worked on at a governmental level that should be consider in the context of your future usage.

More control: As previously mentioned, one of the biggest benefits of a blockchain is its ability to function completely autonomously. However, due to the fact that bitcoin then allowed for near-anonymous transactions, it made it very easy for those with an interest in avoiding the law to do so. As cryptocurrency becomes more well-known, regulatory and governmental agencies including the Securities and Exchange Commission, Department of Homeland Security, FBI, and the Financial Crimes Enforcement Network, just in the US, have all started becoming more interested in its potential for unlawful activities.

Scrutiny began to increase during 2013 when the Financial Crimes Enforcement Network decided that cryptocurrency exchanges represented a form of an existing money service business. This meant that they would then fall under government regulations. DHS quickly took advantage of this fact to freeze the accounts of Mt. Gox, the biggest bitcoin exchange in the world at this time based on accusations of money laundering.

This was then followed up with a more recent SEC ruling to deny bitcoin the ability to open an official cryptocurrency exchange trade fund. This move led to a decrease in the price of bitcoin, though that decrease was then countered by an even stronger increase. The denial of this application was still pending review as of September 2017. This then places cryptocurrencies into a bit of an odd situation as their increasing levels of scrutiny makes it harder for them to follow through on their purpose, despite being more popular than ever.

If cryptocurrency is every going to reach a truly mainstream level, and be absorbed into existing financial systems then it needs to find a way to remain true to its initial purpose while also becoming complex enough to hold off the security threats it is sure to face in the future. What's more, it will also need to become simple enough that the average person can use it without issue. Finally, it would need to remain decentralized enough to still be recognizable, while also including various checks and balances to prevent misuse when it comes to things like money laundering or tax evasion. Taken together, this makes it likely that the successful blockchain of the future is going to be some sort of amalgamation of the current form and a more traditional currency.

United States: The United States government is currently working hard to crack down on those who are using blockchain as a means to launder money. They aren't going to be content with that level of control for long, it seems, as signs point to the fact that they are currently working on their own blockchain based cryptocurrency known as Fedcoin. The idea here is that the Federal Reserve could generate a unique cryptocurrency quite easily. The only difference between the blockchain they create and any other is the fact that it would allow for the Federal Reserve to retain the power to go in an remove transactions that they don't approve of.

The rollout of the Fedcoin would occur after the genesis block were created and the rate of Fedcoins being set to 1 to 1 with the dollar. Over time, it would become more and more difficult to come across regular dollars until they were phased out entirely. This would then ultimately lead to a type of cryptocurrency that is both decentralized for its individual transactions, and centralized when it comes to things like limiting available supply and keeping an eye on all types of transactions.

The Federal Reserve is already on its way towards making this plan a reality, so much so that they hosted a closed-door meeting with bitcoin authorities in the fall of 2016. The Chair of the Federal Reserve sat in on the meeting in person, along with representatives from the Bank for International Settlements, World Bank and the International Monetary Fund. During this meeting, one of the talks was literally titled Why Central Banks Will Issue Digital Currencies.

Russia: Russia issued a dramatic shift in its cryptocurrency polices in 2017. Prior to this point anyone caught using cryptocurrency could face jail time, now however the country is embracing digital currency wholeheartedly. The reason for this is related to the extreme level of corruption that Russia has seen in its banking sector over the past several years. More than one hundred banks have been closed in the past three years, and a rash of money laundering schemes still can't be stopped.

To better track where its money is going, the Russian government is currently working on several blockchain based technical applications that will make it easier for them to monitor real time transactions. This makes it appear as though they are less interested in creating a new digital currency and are instead more interested in the distributed ledger portion of the blockchain technology. There is currently no word yet on if Russia plans to create a new blockchain or utilize an existing blockchain for its own ends.

China: China is currently a major supporter in the blockchain space. In June of 2017, the People's Bank of China released and official news report regarding the creation of its own type of digital currency with the ability to scale dramatically depending on the number of transactions that are seen per day. While all of the details have not yet been released, various sources seem to indicate that the bank could release the currency to the world alongside its renminbi project. While no firm release date is forthcoming, the currency is already well underway in the development process and has already seeing testing amongst many of the country's commercial banks and the People's Bank. This testing is a huge step forward for officially sanctioned cryptocurrencies and blockchains of all types. It also proves how committed China is to the idea of thoroughly exploring the digital currency space.

The digital currency they are creating is likely to cause major gains for their economy overall. This is due to the fact that it is back by the People's Bank which means it is functionally the same as a bank note with far fewer associated fees. It would also do a good deal when it comes to bringing banking in China to the modern age as many of its citizens do not have access to traditional banking services.

Chapter 3: Cryptocurrency and Blockchain Interactions

While blockchain is poised to do a great many different things in the near future, for now the most important thing you are going to want to keep in mind is that blockchains make cryptocurrency possible, and bitcoin jumped in price more than $2,000 during the summer of 2017. While this price has pushed it out of the league of many amateur investors, there are more than 1,000 different cryptocurrencies on the market these days so there are plenty of opportunities out there for those who are interested in a potentially profitable investment. This is not to say that there isn't risk involved as well, however, so it is important to keep the risks of cryptocurrency investment in mind as well before making any investments in the space.

Pros

Lowers risk of identity theft: As cryptocurrencies are purely digital, they are naturally susceptible to far less risk than traditional types of currency. They cannot be forged or counterfeited and the transaction cannot be manipulated so that it never happened do to the underlying blockchain. Additionally, once you have bought into a cryptocurrency you can move it about freely without have to worry about transactions with specious companies or individuals putting your details in places they would rather not be. Instead, with most exchanges if you already own cryptocurrency there is no type of verification whatsoever. With most exchanges, without cryptocurrency in hand, you need to generate a new debit or credit transaction with each round of funding.

Easy access: There are roughly 3.5 billion people who have some type of internet access and also do not have any reliable form of banking. This is a niche that the cryptocurrency market is looking to take advantage of to the fullest, and is expected to cause significant growth in the industry as it becomes more commonplace. Assuming this type of banking catches on, then those who invest in cryptocurrency early are going to see more than just a profit, they could potentially see profit on a significant scale.

Low cost: While every cryptocurrency interaction involves a transaction fee, the fees for making this type of exchange is still generally lower than making an exchange on a traditional broker website.

Cons

New technology: While bitcoin has been a quality investment for the past few years, the cryptocurrency market as a whole is still extremely untested overall which means that many of its risks are still very poorly defined, especially when compared to more traditional markets. This naturally makes the highs in the market more dramatic than similar markets, but it also makes the lowers much more dramatic as well. There are no guarantees when one is going to become the other, trends can come and go in completely unpredictable patterns that no one has seen before. What it all comes down to is that there just is not enough information available to be able to accurately predict where the market is going to be in a year, much less five. Until the market stabilizes somewhat, there is no way of telling if every dollar you invest is going to be worth $2, one year from now or if it is going to be worth $.02.

Extreme volatility: Bitcoin, the most stable of all of the cryptocurrencies, is still five time more volatile than gold and has nearly seven times more volatility than if you were to invest that money into the S&P 500. While volatility means a greater chance at profit, it also means the chance at a loss is going to be much higher than it would otherwise be. It is also important to understand that most of the purchases of cryptocurrency that are made, are done for speculative purposes. This means that the currency is being purchased by investors, not people who are actually planning to use it on a day-to-day basis. This, in turn means that prices are likely to rise higher than a true supply and demand market would indicate. This early adopter phenomenon means those who buy in early are going to experience a nice price increase, but the upward movement ultimately won't last. This isn't a question of if, it is a question of when.

Lack of physicality: While the fact that cryptocurrency is a digital means of payment is one of its leading characteristics, the fact remains that this concept does present some challenges. Specifically, consider the fact that if the server holding your cryptocurrency goes down, and there is no backup, then your investment is gone forever. You can take a variety of methods to put the control of your cryptocurrency in your hands, but the fact remains that a real coin is always going to be easier to hold onto than a digital one.

The vast potential for profit when it comes to hacking into a blockchain also means that hackers are never going to stop trying to do just that. What this also means, is that they are occasionally going to be successful. For example, the Ethereum platform has seen a variety of different attacks throughout its lifetime, one of which was so successful that it necessitated a hard fork that saw the Ethereum blockchain divided into those that saw a profit from the attack and those who lost out because of it. A split in the value of the dollar is never going to occur, no matter how many are stolen in a bank robbery which just proves how unpredictable investing in a new opportunity can be.

Trading cryptocurrency

Regardless of how familiar you are with trading traditional securities, trading in the cryptocurrency market can prove to be extremely profitable, as long as you have come to terms with the potential for risk. Don't forget, it is important to never invest any money that you can't afford to lose. There is very little barrier to entry, as previously mentioned, if you already have cryptocurrency then you won't even need to worry about verifying your account.

Another useful thing about trading in this market is the fact that there are no centralized exchanges which means it is every exchange for itself. This then leads to a market that is very fragmented, which means it naturally produces spreads that are much wider than you are likely to see anywhere else. This lack of regulation also means it is often quite easy to find a very large margin which means that small investments have the potential to become large returns faster than with virtually all other types of investment, though the same can be said about losses as well. Finally, depending on the cryptocurrency you are trading in, you will likely be able to find it for different rates on different exchanges which means you might be able to make a profit simply by purchasing them in one place and selling them somewhere else.

The most common way to trade cryptocurrencies through a trading company is with a contract for differences. This type of contract binds the buyer and seller together for the length of the contract, once it ends, the buyer will pay the seller the difference between the price of the asset at the end of the contract and what it was at the start. If the price moves the other way then the seller has to pay the buyer the difference. When it comes to securing leverage, you will likely be able to find rates in excess of 20 to 1, though it is not recommended that you seek them out until you are very familiar with what it is like to trade in this market.

Global currency: When it comes to standard currency, the number of things that can influence the price is naturally going to be fairly limited. The opposite is true for cryptocurrencies, however, and it is difficult to tell what is going to set investors off before it happens. Any currency news anywhere has the potential to set prices shifting dramatically, in fact, several of bitcoin's most significant moves have come about due to the introduction to controls for capital in Greece and when China devalued the Yuan.

Market always ready: While the forex market is traditionally thought of as the most robust market as it is open 120 hours each week, the cryptocurrency market is open 168 hours each week, and trades are always happening regardless of what part of the world is currently active. Currently there are about 100 major cryptocurrency exchanges in the world who all offer various levels of trading along with differing rates based on their level of service. As such, it should not take more than a little research to find the one that is right for you.

This can also be seen as a negative, depending on your tolerance for risk as these factors can be enough to generate large swings on a daily basis. In fact, price shifts of more than 5 percent are common on most days for the larger cryptocurrencies and the smaller ones aren't surprised if they see 15 percent movement or more.

Finding your exchange

When it comes to committing to a specific exchange, it is important to always do the relevant research that you need in order to feel comfortable about your choice. Moving forward without doing enough research can cause you to end up in a situation where you exchange suddenly disappears with your money or you find out that it doesn't have the funds to cover all of its obligations and there is a run on it as everyone tries to get their money back at once. If this sort of thing were to happen, it is important to keep in mind that you are going to have very little recourse, especially if you choose an exchange that is not based in your country. This is why the initial choice you make has the potential to be so impactful.

Prioritize transparent exchanges: As a general rule, the more transparent the exchange you choose is willing to be, the more on the level it is going to be. This means you are going to want to be able to take a look at their order book, which is just a version of their distributed ledger and shows how much of everything is being bought or sold on a regular basis. You should also be able to request details regarding where their funds are held and their system for verifying their appropriate level of reserve currency. If you have a hard time getting answers to these very basic questions then the exchange might simply not have the means to make that information public. On the other hand, it could mean that they are a fractional exchange and can't cover their debts. When it comes to choosing the right cryptocurrency exchange it is always better to be safe than sorry.

Available security: It is very important to always choose an exchange with a healthy level of security, after all, as previously mentioned your cryptocurrency profits won't exist outside this exchange without your help which means security is of the upmost importance. You will only want to use exchanges that have an HTTPS in front of their URL as this indicates they are operating off of a secure protocol which means they are actively working to keep your account details from being stolen. You will also want to ensure that the exchange is utilizing a type of two-factor authentication in addition to standard secure login practices. If your exchange isn't at least this well protected then you are flirting with theft of both your identity and your investments.

Fees add up: Almost every type of cryptocurrency has an associated fee that is paid, part of which goes to the blockchain platform holder and part goes to the miner or miners who verify your transaction. While these fees are certainly voluntary, in most cases, not paying them removes much of the incentive for your transaction to be verified which means the entire process might end up taking longer than it otherwise would. Unless you choose an exchange in China, you will then also have to pay a transaction fee to the exchange as well. With so many fees flying around, they can add up quickly which means you are always going to have a trading plan in place before you make your first trade to prevent yourself from losing a sizeable portion of your trading capital to fees.

Try for something local: Despite the fact that there are cryptocurrency exchanges worldwide, you should aim for one that operates in your home country if possible. This is advantageous in multiple ways, the first of which is that you will naturally be able to take advantage of periods of higher volume simply because you will be on the same general time zone as your exchange. Choosing a local option will also make it easier should you ever need to contact support, and your deposits will go through more quickly as well. Even better, depending on your country and its laws, there might even be some type of oversight regarding cryptocurrency exchanges which means getting your money back after some funny business might not be completely out of the question.

When choosing a local exchange, make sure to verify they offer the cryptocurrency pairs that you are looking for. Exchanges vary dramatically from one to the next so there are no guarantees you will even be able to trade in your local currency, even if you pick an exchange that is close to home.

Understand transaction times: As all cryptocurrency transaction need to be verified and added to the blockchain before they can clear, exchanges often work on a bit of a lead time to let this process breathe. It is important that you choose an exchange whose transaction time is reasonable, for the best results. Likewise, you are going to want to ensure that the price you buy at is the price that is locked in regardless of how long the transaction takes. If this is not the case then you risk making a trade that looks promising, only to have the price change and ruin everything before it actually goes through.

Well-known exchanges

Kraken: This is a European exchange that handles the highest volume of euro trades each day. They are also within the top 15 when it comes to USD exchanges as well.

Coinbase: This is the elder statesman of the cryptocurrency exchanges in the US and has the honor of being the oldest continuously active USD exchange. It is known for being strictly regulated and is still one of the top five when it comes to pure volume traded per day.

OKCoin: This is primarily a USD exchange that is based in Japan which means it is subject to far fewer regulations than most of the other exchanges in this list. If you are looking for higher margins and few fees, and are comfortable with the extra risk, then this is the exchange for you.

Bitstamp: This exchange has been running continuously since 2011 and the second most commonly used USD exchange with a volume greater than 10,000 units a day.

Bitfinex: This exchange does the greatest amount of USD trading by volume of all the exchanges, worldwide, clearing more than 200,000 units of cryptocurrency every single week. If you are interested in going with this option, be aware that if you already own cryptocurrency then you can get started without submitting to any type of verification.

Initial coin offerings (ICOs)

In 2017, a blockchain based company managed to raise more than $150 million in less than 24 hours and another, Status.im managed half that amount. These outpourings of investor generosity are known as initial coin offerings and, like everything having to do with cryptocurrency, they offer a heavy risk in exchange for a potentially lucrative reward. As of summer, 2017, the process had already raised nearly $500,000,000.

Despite being a play on the term initial public offering, the initial coin offering is actually a very different beast in almost every way. An initial coin offering is really just another crowdfunding strategy where a blockchain company offers its new cryptocurrency at a very investor-friendly rate and then investors buy it up in hopes of seeing the price rise even as little as 50 cents. The company then, in theory at least, will have the money to complete its project and come to market, where its products or services will be so widely adopted that the price of its cryptocurrency will rise based on increased demand. The Ethereum platform has quickly proven itself the most popular home for companies who are looking to offer an initial coin offering.

A majority of this money currently comes from China, though investors from around the world have been known to open their checkbooks if the price is right. While investing on what is more or less an unknown quantity always comes with certain risks, initial coin offerings are even riskier still. This is due to the fact that they are not currently under the SEC regulatory umbrella which means their business plans are not put through the same testing that those who apply for an initial public offering are. There is also some concern that the success that the first few initial coin offerings garnered is actually due to another bubble which means it is unlikely to last.

While they do have issues, initial coin offerings also have the potential to generate serious profits for investors who make the right decisions at the right times. Nevertheless, if you are considering this type of investment then you need to understand that if you choose to invest in an initial coin offering, then you are making one of the riskiest investments possible.

To counteract the potential danger as much as possible, you will need to approach all initial coin offerings with a quizzical mindset and the first thing you will want to do is look through any information the company has made available including, hopefully, a business plan. This will make it easier for you to determine if a specific project makes sense on a financial level and to ensure that is business proposition checks out in the long-term. You will also need to know that the market is going to actually want the product or service the company is hoping to provide. Furthermore, you will want to double check and see what the role of the cryptocurrency that you are buying into will be when the product or service is up and running.

You will also need to keep in mind that buying into an initial coin offering is going to be quite different than buying into an initial public offering. When buying into the latter, you come away with ownership shares that essentially mean you own a small portion of the company in question. Initial coin offerings grant you no such rights, just a pile of digital currency that may or may not eventually be worth something. Additionally, initial public offerings have stricter requirements placed on them including accreditation obligations and fiduciary requirements that the company must meet before it can have its offering, none of which is required for initial coin offerings.

In reality, you are likely never going to see more than a whitepaper, business plan and website from an initial coin offering company, and sometimes not even all of these. They are more than likely not going to have a product or prototype to show off either which means you are going to be taking a lot of what is being told to you on faith. You also need to be aware that just because an initial coin offering sees a good amount of response early on, doesn't mean this goodwill will last until its launch day, much less beyond it. Also noteworthy is the fact that many analysts believe that giving new companies too much money too soon actually limits their potential as the owner's feel the need to spend all the money available to them while feeling less inclined to actually complete a usable product.

While the list of poor ICOs ranges from those with overly optimistic ideas to downright scams with the sole goal of taking your hard earned cash. There are an increasing number of ICOs out there with nothing more than a flashy website filled with a ton of buzzwords and a high valuation based on nothing more than their own opinion. The single biggest factor you should examine before investing is the real world viability of the project. What solution to a current problem does the company promise to solve? Even more so, is there even a problem in the first place that requires blockchain technology? It's important to examine the team behind the project, and more importantly their previous track record with projects like it. Another main determinant should be whether the token they are offering has actual utility for the project, or are investors just going to dump it for a quick profit as soon as it hits the open market? You should also watch out for any huge bonuses offered for early investors. It's not uncommon for a pre-sale bonus to be offered, but if these bonuses top 100%, you can and should question what the incentive is for non-early adopters, and if the team are just trying to generate as much cash as quickly as possible. One advantage the Ethereum platform does have is the ability for smart contracts to be coded into the ICO, such as funds held in a service similar to escrow, to ensure they are returned to investors if the project founders do not uphold their end of the agreement.

Last but not least, it is worth noting that a majority of the currently successful initial coin offerings have been based on the Ethereum blockchain platform which means the basis of these companies is still essentially an untested technology. While the Ethereum blockchain platform has a better chance of making it than making it than most, the fact of the matter is that it is still untested technology so there is still downside potential as well as upside. Overall, it might be the best choice to instead wait and see how the first round of initial coin offering companies pan out before getting too involved with these types of investments directly.

Tips for investing successfully

While starting to invest in cryptocurrency is as easy as finding an exchange and putting some money into the cryptocurrency machine, doing so and turning an investment profit is something else completely. What's next is a list of things you will want to keep in mind in order to invest successfully in the long-term.

It's a commodity: The first thing you are going to need to do is to think about cryptocurrency in the same way you would any other commodity. Just like any other commodity, cryptocurrency is used for practical as well as investment purposes, just as precious metals have commercial uses and base metals have industrial ones. Additionally, they are all trade through exchanges that more or less all follow the same rules. This means that in order to choose a cryptocurrency that is likely to increase in value, you are going to want to pick the one that is likely to provide the most real-world value or has the greatest number of probable uses beyond just P2P transactions.

Increasing usage: When gathered together as a whole, all the currently existing cryptocurrencies have a market cap of about $160 billion. This puts them in the same league as companies like Tesla and Microsoft in terms of pure numbers. What makes this number particularly interesting is that real world usage and increasing market cap have gone hand in hand so far, and reports show that blockchain and cryptocurrency usage is only likely to increase for at least the next five years.

This is when market saturation is expected to occur and is likely when many of the existing bubbles break for the first time. Nevertheless, while the market is still extremely volatile in the short-term, cryptocurrency as a long-term investment should be relatively reliable. When this number is looked at through the lens of the current market cap then the potential for growth is truly staggering. Essentially the price of cryptocurrency across the board has nowhere to go but up. Even better, once the number of users eventually stabilizes, investor won't have to worry about the bubble effect nearly as much because prices will likely stop decreasing dramatically at that point as well.

Point in the cycle: The market cycle is a type of investment pattern that every investment goes through sooner or later. On the positive side, it starts with optimism before moving up to thrill, and then peaking with euphoria. It then decreases through anxiety, denial, fear, depression and finally, panic. After it bottoms out it then rises back up through depression, hope and relief before once again reaching optimism.

While bitcoin has already been through the cycle more than once, most recently bottoming out during the 2014 crash, the vast majority of all cryptocurrencies are still very much in the optimism stage so there is still plenty of time to get in while the getting is good. As long as you do your research correctly in the first place there is no reason you couldn't realistically see five reliable years of growth on your investment before it hits the euphoria stage.

While this is decidedly good news, it is also important to keep in mind the fact that the cryptocurrency market today, is very much the same as the dotcom boom of the 90s. What this means, is that roughly 80 percent of all the cryptocurrencies on the market today are going to fail before or during the period when the market hits its saturation point. This is due to the fact that there will only be so many options in a limited marketplace that only a handful will be able to survive the buildup. Many investors will end up throwing their money at a company without having any idea what that company actually does and the market will crumble because of it, though if you know what's coming you will be able to avoid the worst of it.

Solving problems is key: It doesn't matter what the potential for profit on a given cryptocurrency turns out to be, buying into it and then sitting back to wait for the magic to happen will never be the most effective money-making strategy. Instead, you will be better served putting time into finding those cryptocurrencies that solve problems for individual markets or, even better, the world at large. The bigger the problem being solved, the more likely it will turn into something that is worth investing in for the long-term. It is especially important to consider solutions when it comes to the banking services that some parts of the world take for granted. Cryptocurrencies that focus on solutions when it comes to making payments and wiring money are going to be good bets in the near future.

Long-term view: Given the amount of movement you can expect to see on a regular basis, the ideal cryptocurrency portfolio is going to be one that focuses solely on the long-term. You are also going to want to make a point of picking several different cryptocurrencies to invest in, between three or five, so that you will never be too negatively affected by serious drops in one place or another. More than anything else it is going to be important that you control your emotions as thoroughly as possible and strive to avoid rash decisions when investments are on the line. When you are first getting started it is a good idea to not watch your investments too closely, as they are likely going to be all over the place. Don't forget, the goal to long-term investing is a steady overall upward trend which means a little back and forth is to be expected.

It is also important to remember that cryptocurrencies do not come with the lock-in risk that many other long-term investments do. If you feel that a certain cryptocurrency's time has come, you can quickly and easily exchange it with any other currency you choose, instead of having to go through the hassle of trading in a more traditional fashion during a down market. As such, you may want to think about investing in cryptocurrency as just keeping money in a savings account, but one that has a much higher potential for return on your primary investment.

Conclusion

Thank you for reading, let's the book was informative and able to provide you with all of the tools you need to achieve your goals, whatever it is that they may be. Just because you've finished this book doesn't mean there is nothing left to learn on the topic, expanding your horizons is the only way to find the mastery you seek.

This is especially true for the blockchain market as it is a new enough technology as to literally be always changing. Only by making it a habit to become a lifelong learner will you ever truly get a grasp on it that you will be able to use for your advantage. Whatever you do, always keep in mind that the market is heading towards an inevitable saturation point which means however you decide to interact with blockchain technology you need to ensure you end up on the right side of it.

It is extremely likely that you will not see another technology this disruptive in your lifetime, and with so many technology variations and cryptocurrencies all vying for the market at once, all you need to do is be aware of the possibility of success to be able to seek it out and reap all the related rewards. It also means that there are plenty of ways to fail, however, so you are going to really need to do your homework and ensure that you never make a move without taking all of your options into consideration fist. Remember, investing in blockchain technology is investing in the long-term, slow and steady wins the race.

Finally, if you found this book useful in anyway, a review on Amazon is always appreciated!